Become an outward-reaching congregation with these *Get Their Name* resources!

Get Their Name Workbook

This is a chapter-by-chapter companion to the book *Get Their Name*. The workbook helps readers to study and reflect on the information and ideas in the book. It focuses on helping readers understand the *Get Their Name* approach to faith sharing.

This resource is for individuals and groups and can be done at your own pace. It's great for church leaders and members.

Get Their Name Study Plus Sermon and Worship Series

This is a two-phase experience for church leaders and members who want to see their churches become growing, outwardly focused communities of faith.

The first phase is a group **Study** for leaders and active members of the church. The 4-part, interactive study focuses on helping leaders to implement the *Get Their Name* approach in their own church. It includes a video conversation starter for each week, available on DVD.

The *Coordinator's Guide* is a complete guide for the pastor or other church leader seeking to facilitate the 4-part *Get Their Name* study plus the 4-week Sermon and Worship series.

The *Participant Workbook* is a complete workbook for those participating in the study.

A Facilitator's Guide is available for free download online. This easy-to-use guide provides all the information needed to lead the *Get Their Name* study.

The *Get Their Name* **DVD** includes a conversation starter video for each of the four sessions, plus a promotional video to use as a tool for inviting people to join the study.

The second phase of the *Get Their Name* experience is a downloadable **Sermon and Worship Series**. This 4-week series is for pastors and other leaders who want to go even deeper, to involve the entire congregation in this life- and church-changing approach to evangelism. Worship helps and full sermon outlines, plus sermon illustration videos and printable promotional materials, are available online.

I thank God for the gift of this book! The authors offer practical, grace-filled training, helping to grow true Wesleyan witnesses in virtually every church setting. I enthusiastically recommend *Get Their Name* for use in both lay and clergy training.

—Bishop Mike Lowry, Bishop of the Central Texas Conference of the United Methodist Church

Get Their Name touches a nerve, intentionally! It will light a fire under clergy and laity, stimulating creative ideas for reaching people.

—Jim Ozier, New Church Development and Congregational Transformation, North Texas Conference, UMC

This is a must-read for people who want to multiply their congregation's impact. *Get Their Name* is a practical, interactive guide for building relationships with our neighbors. The authors keep it simple, focused, and practical.

—Paul Nixon and Christie Latona, Founders of Readiness360.org

Farr, Anderson, and Kotan share powerful steps that Christians everywhere can use and apply. This book is a wonderful resource for individuals and small groups.

—Ken Willard, Director of Leadership Training and Development, Leadership4Transformation

The tools and detailed instructions provided in this book illuminate a pathway to Kingdom beauty . . . making disciples of Jesus Christ for transformation of the world.

—Larry Fagan, Eldecon Inc.

Get Their Name fills a huge gap for evangelism in today's world. This excellent material helps cure our strong resistance to the "E" word, and it helps us to make new disciples. It is a must for any pastor or laity leader in today's church.

—Dr. David P. Hyatt, Leadership4Transformation, Healthy Church Initiative, Missouri Conference, UMC

Bob, Doug, and Kay remind us of the need for intentional, missional plans for our lives and churches. They give us practical tools for engaging with the world and sharing the good news in straightforward, do-able actions!

—Rev. Karen Koons Hayden, Director of Pastoral Excellence, Missouri Conference, UMC

Get Their Name brings wisdom, experience, and insight. It's a great tool for churches wanting to find a new way to answer their call.

—Sherry Habben, Director of Connectional Ministries, Missouri Conference, UMC

GET THEIR NAME

Grow Your Church
by Building New Relationships

BOB FARR
DOUG ANDERSON
KAY KOTAN

Abingdon Press™

Nashville

Get Their Name

Grow Your Church By Building New Relationships

Copyright © 2013 by Abingdon Press

Library of Congress Cataloging-in-Publication Data

Farr, Bob.
    Get their name : grow your church by building new relationships / Bob Farr, Doug Anderson, Kay Kotan.
        1 online resource.
    Includes bibliographical references and index.
    Description based on print version record and CIP data provided by publisher; resource not viewed.
        ISBN 978-1-4267-7111-8 (epub)—ISBN 978-1-4267-5931-4 (pbk. / trade pbk. : alk. paper) 1. Witness bearing (Christianity) 2. Interpersonal relations—Religious aspects—Christianity. 3. Church growth. I. Anderson, Douglas T., 1951- II. Kotan, Kay. III. Title.
    BV4520
    254'.5.—dc23

                                                                            2013016717

13 14 15 16 17 18 19 20 21—10 9 8 7 6 5 4 3 2 1

MANUFACTURED IN THE UNITED STATES OF AMERICA

We would like to extend our love and appreciation to our families for their relentless support of our ministries. We would also like to thank the following for their contributions in many ways to the thoughts, ideas, and passion for this topic: Bishop Robert Schnase, Dr. David Hyatt, Ken Willard, Tammy Calcote, The Missouri Annual Conference of the United Methodist Church. To those pastors and laity alike who have been willing to create a culture of experimentation and for their willingness to try new things.

CONTENTS

PREFACE

After consulting with more than four hundred churches throughout the country, we have observed that the primary focus for most evangelism effort is on recovering inactive members. Evangelism becomes passive, waiting for them to come, being polite when they arrive, helping them to join our organization, and then trying to get them to come back if they quit attending worship or giving money. This hands-off style of evangelism is not working—and has not worked for more than fifty years!

We worked with a church that launched a new worship service to reach those not already connected to the Christian faith. To connect with persons who were not involved in any church, the pastor passionately urged those already actively attending worship to invite others in their relational network to come to a social event designed to reach out to those not already Christian. One young man who had grown up in the church and its passive culture of private faith not only refused to invite anyone but was adamant that he would not even attend if inviting others was the expectation. He didn't do that, and he wouldn't do that!

This book is about helping people in our churches move past the fear of inviting or sharing faith with others and move toward an active, passionate missionary lifestyle. We must recapture our missionary soul as professing Christians in America. This is primarily a book about how to learn what we have been afraid or ill equipped to do.

We can't keep waiting for people to arrive at our doors. We have done this for too many years. This passive behavior goes against the missional roots of our Christian faith. We have gone from being outwardly focused to being inwardly centered. This static and inward passivity won't work in a secular world where the gospel must be actively demonstrated to be communicated.

Four observations offer a rationale for this book.

OBSERVATION ONE

Inwardly focused churches tend to define and practice evangelism as "reconnecting disconnected church folks."

OBSERVATION TWO

Outwardly focused churches define and practice evangelism as connecting the unconnected folks to Jesus and then to the church.

OBSERVATION THREE

The pool of churched people to connect with is dramatically shrinking, while the pool of the unchurched, never-connected population is growing exponentially. This is especially true among the millennial generation.

OBSERVATION FOUR

Early denominational movements focused on unconnected folks, while the established churches of the day focused on and supported the folks who were already churched when they arrived in America. These movements became institutional over time, and they focused on membership rather than discipleship. The mainline churches were dislodged from the center of American culture by the upheaval of the 1960s. The situation became further confused by the resulting rise of religious conservatism in the 1970s and 1980s. This led to the American polarization of religious liberals and religious conservatives, which in turn led to the disaffection of youth from religion in the 1990s and 2000s. The mainline churches as a result are bewildered and unsure about how to proceed through an accelerated state of decline.

CONSEQUENCE

If any denomination is to have a future, it must reconnect to the biblical purpose and mission of making *new* disciples of Jesus Christ for the transformation of the world. To accomplish this mission, it requires us to be once again people who widely, continually, and fervently share their faith in Jesus Christ with those who do not yet have such a faith. This sharing must occur in relevant ways, without being obnoxious, so that they might have the possibility to come to this life-transforming and saving faith.

FIND YOUR OWN
FAITH STORY
AND SHARE IT

Most Christians rarely share their faith in Jesus Christ with other persons—especially persons who are not yet followers of Jesus Christ. And yet this is our central task. So why is this lack of faith sharing so prevalent? A family tree explains what seems to happen in many generations.

In our grandmothers' generation, born one hundred years ago, 80 percent of people were connected to God through church—and if Protestant, the vast majority was part of the older established Protestant churches. Of the generation born eighty years ago, 65 percent are still connected to God through church, with the majority in an older, established Protestant church. In the Baby Boomer generation, born sixty years ago, fewer than 35 percent are connected to God through church, and if Protestant, the majority is not in an older, established (mainline) Protestant church. Of the Generation X children, born thirty to forty years ago, fewer than 20 percent are connected to God through church, and of those who are Protestant, a strong majority is not in a mainline Protestant church. Among the Millennials (children born in the past ten to twenty years), fewer than 10 percent will be connected to God through church—and if Protestant, the vast majority will not be in a mainline Protestant church. With each successive generation, the number of persons connecting to God through the church is dropping significantly, as is the percentage that is connecting with an older, established Protestant

1

church. This trend is the result, in part, of how we have defined and practiced evangelism for five or more generations. Mainline Protestants have understood evangelism as reconnecting disconnected churched people who come through our church doors. In other words, our evangelism has been waiting on folks to arrive who are already Christian but are disconnected from a church home.

It is a long-held fantasy that those who left the church for college would one day return, after graduation and marriage, when they started their family. When our grandparents followed this pattern, the period between leaving for college and returning to church was just a gap of a few years. If our parents followed this pattern, the time gap in leaving for college and returning as a new parent would be about five years. Today, if our young people follow that pattern, the gap could be ten to twelve years or more. These young people have now spent more than half of their lives outside the church. They are out of the routine of attending church, which makes it much more difficult to get back to church, especially in this secular world that is pulling them further away from the church. In fact, those who do return to the church usually do so because they have moved to the area or have married someone who is already a member of a church. Our current system is based on an effort to connect with Christians. This system isn't working well. Additionally, we don't even have a strategy to connect with the unchurched.

PATRICK'S STORY

The teenager sat in the pew wanting the service to be over more than anything else. He wanted to get back to his friends on Facebook and through texting. He came to service only because his mother dragged him to this memorial service where the names of his recently deceased grandfather and aunt would be read. Patrick had been attending parochial school for twelve years. Yet, when communion was served, he sat quietly in the pew without moving. Of course, once the family was driving home, his mother inquired why he chose not to partake in communion. Patrick proceeded to explain to his mother that he just wasn't sure that he "believed." His mother was crushed and angry. Her anger was a result of her feelings that his actions were disrespectful to his grandmother, who was in attendance. She further explained that she couldn't believe that she had invested in an expensive twelve-year parochial education and he was now questioning if he believed! How could he! How ungrateful this teenager was for his parents' financial investment. The sad part is the anger was not about the concern of her son not having an authentic relationship with God. It was instead the fact that her financial investment did not create his unquestioned religious affiliation. It just never occurred to her to be upset about his lacking personal relationship with God!

Rarely have mainline Protestant churches focused on reaching persons who are not already connected to Jesus Christ in a vital faith and helping them come to that life-transforming relationship with Jesus Christ.

Yet there are pockets of churches, denominational and nondenominational, that are growing significantly and affecting their communities. And why? These churches grow and affect their communities because they have defined and practiced evangelism over the last five or more generations. These churches by and large understand evangelism as connecting persons to God through Jesus Christ in a vital, dynamic, personal relationship of faith. And over the past five generations, the number of persons to be reached for Jesus Christ in this mission field continues to grow dramatically. Or as Jesus put it so well, "The harvest is bigger than you can imagine, but there are few workers" (Luke 10:2). Evangelism is about building authentic relationships with people we don't know. This relationship might lead to a conversation, which might lead to an invitation to gather with a community of faith, which might lead to an authentic relationship with Christ. Instead of simply sitting back and waiting for people to come to us.

> **Evangelism = Building authentic relationships with people we don't know.**

But how do we equip churched people to practice with competence and confidence this new style of relational evangelism? This effort requires a step-by-step process over the course of two or more years. This is a major cultural shift, from promoting membership to becoming personal missionaries. A two-year process is not an easy answer, but there is hope.

Of course, we don't like to do evangelism! We did not grow up practicing relational evangelism. We will discover a process that starts basic and then progresses a step at a time to equip persons to share their faith competently and confidently. So let's now begin to unpack exactly what that process looks like and how to implement each step in this process with the persons in our own congregations.

Chapter

FAITH SHARING IN SERVICE

Let's begin with our analogy of elementary relational evangelism. *Elementary*, of course, refers to something that is very basic. Elementary relational evangelism, then, will be fairly easy for us to do. It is something that we are familiar with, and it doesn't stretch us too far out of our comfort zone. In other words, it's a good basic first step in finding and sharing our faith.

Relational evangelism is rooted in our practice of service. Many mainline churches across the country are doing an outstanding job of serving persons in their communities and regions, and across the globe. This service is an important demonstration of God's love. It has unmistakable intrinsic value in and of itself. But very few persons are connected to Jesus Christ and Christ's church as a result of service alone. Providing food through a pantry is an important and needed ministry. But rarely will the persons served connect with Christ or the church as a result of that service. So, while we love doing good deeds, we are not so good at adding the Good Word to the good deeds. Relational evangelism will teach us to add the Good Word to the good deed. Let's look at the difference between service and relational evangelism through service.

GOOD DEED + GOOD WORD = GOOD NEWS

Elementary relational evangelism centers on serving others. It is significantly different from service alone. We can illustrate this best with an extended example. Let's say that this summer you decide that you will again distribute cold water bottles to persons attending the fair, festival, or celebration in your community or area. But instead of doing this simply as a matter of service, you decide that this year you're going to do this as active relational evangelism through service. Instead of just handing out the water bottles from a booth marked "Shady Creek United Methodist Church," each water bottle will have a simple card attached by a rubber band. The card communicates two important messages. The first might read something like this: "This bottle of cold water is a free gift from your friends at Shady Creek United Methodist Church. This is our way of sharing with you and showing you God's love, because God's love is always free and is available all the time to everyone, including you." This is the heart of the first important message: God loves you, and that love is free all the time for everyone. This is a key component of relational evangelism through service. It must include the evangel, the "Good News." So the water bottle becomes an example and demonstration of the Good News of God's love.

Your chicken noodle dinner for missions that you charge for cannot be relational evangelism through service, because it is not free and therefore not an example of God's free love, which is the Good News. Let's be clear on the distinction between a fundraiser and relational evangelism through service. We advise you to limit your church to no more than two or three fundraisers (if any) a year. It is bad theology to raise money from the very people we are trying to reach for Jesus Christ in the mission field. This leaves a bad taste in the mouth! The biblical understanding of resourcing the church is simply tithing by those who already believe in Jesus Christ. Fundraising is a civic response to a need.

Hand out things to hand out.

Let's return to the example of the bottled water and examine the second message: "Just like we know that in order to live we need water, we also know that to live fully and deeply, we need to be connected to God who loves us. So if you'd like to experience more of God's love in your life, we would like to invite you to join us in a celebration of God's love in worship this Sunday at 10 a.m. at Shady Creek United Methodist Church (corner of Shady and Creek Avenues). Come celebrate God's love with us this Sunday!" Relational evangelism includes a clear invitation to connect with God and with our church.

In this illustration, the persons we give water to do not know that we are giving them water in order to show them God's love unless we tell them that's the reason. And they don't know that they could experience this God who loves them unless we tell them. And they also don't know that we would love to have them join us in worship celebration unless we tell them. We cannot assume that they understand all of this simply because we handed them a bottle of cold water. For this to be evangelism, that message has to be communicated in a clear, simple, and inviting way.

Relational evangelism through service is connecting service to a clear written communication of the Good News of God's love. Vineyard Christian Fellowship in Cincinnati, Ohio is a church that has developed an outstanding practice of relational evangelism through service, with excellent results. Steve Sjogren was the pastor of the church when this relational evangelism through service was developed. This church practiced a variety of service evangelism projects on a monthly basis, drawing a significant number of persons to the church for worship. Please note that a significant number of people will not come until we first personally go to meet them where they are. Relational evangelism through service does exactly this. As a result of this relational evangelism through service, Vineyard Christian Fellowship grew from under two hundred in average worship attendance to just over one thousand in a period of about ten years. Pastor Sjogren shared the church's experiences and insights in a book entitled *Conspiracy of Kindness.*

We see another example at the United Methodist Church of the Resurrection in downtown Kansas City, Missouri. Pastor Scott Chrostek launched First Serve Saturdays at his new church start-up. For Pastor Scott, First Serve Saturdays served two purposes: it built the reputation of the church as one that serves and cares about downtown Kansas City, and it gave people a place to connect in the first steps of their faith journey, even before attending worship.

The Missouri Conference of the United Methodist Church was so compelled by this example that it conducted a one-day outreach to the mission field on September 11, 2011 dubbed "Serve 2011." More than four hundred churches and ten thousand people participated; 25 percent of the latter were unconnected.

This practice of relational evangelism does not require people to articulate their faith. It simply requires them to demonstrate it by their service. Using our previous example, the card on the water bottle does the explaining. It is important to note that helping others is something that children, youth, and younger adults especially want to engage in. Relational evangelism through service is a great way for these age groups to begin sharing the Good News of God's love in Jesus Christ. In fact, the first connection with the congregation for young people is often through service opportunities. Members of the generation under 30 years of age desire to roll up their sleeves and serve others. There is more about how service projects are a part of the discipleship process in Chapter Ten.

Take a few moments now to reflect on how you might do relational evangelism through service in your church:

- What relational evangelism service projects could you do with your current resources to express God's love to persons in your community?
- How might you modify current service projects so that they function as relational evangelism through service?
- How do you see relational evangelism helping persons in your community discover and experience God's love?
- What difference do you think this would make in transforming your community?
- What difference do you think this would make in transforming your church?

> **We must meet people where they are, not where we are.**

After you've had a significant number of persons in your church practicing relational evangelism through service on a regular basis over the course of several months—congratulations! You are now ready to move into middle school evangelism.

Chapter

FAITH SHARING IN GROUPS

A few years ago, I (Doug) had an extended conversation with an old friend. We shared our mutual observation that very few mainline Christians share their faith with others and pondered together why that was so. Then the obvious struck us both. The reason is that they don't share their faith inside *the church in their small groups. If they are ever going to share their faith outside the church, they must first learn to practice sharing their faith inside the church.*

Middle school is different from elementary school in several important ways. In middle school, you have many teachers rather than just one teacher. You meet in several different classrooms rather than simply staying in one classroom for the entire day. You attend classes with different students in each class rather than the same students all day in the same class. Middle school challenges you to discover your identity, to form your life around that identity, and to build and develop a number of new relationships in new settings. It is more challenging than elementary school, taking us farther out of our comfort zone and expanding our learning and practices.

In the last chapter, we began to get comfortable with meeting new people in relational evangelism through service. We also began to add the Good Word to our good deeds. We began to make simple invitations to church through our service projects. That was elementary evangelism. Next we moved to middle school evangelism. In middle school evangelism, we learn how to share our faith in safe places with people we already know. Step Two is learning to share our faith through small groups, Bible studies, or Sunday school classes. Middle school evangelism is about identity, communication, and relationships. These are also three key elements in rediscovering our faith stories.

It struck us just a few years ago that something had been going on in most small groups, Bible studies, and Sunday school classes for a long time. But we simply didn't see it. In most of these groups, we spend significant time discussing what we think about God, what we understand about God, what we believe about God, what we think about the Bible, and what we understand to be true about the Bible. All of these are excellent things to think about and discuss with one another. Thinking and talking about our understanding of God in the Scriptures is an important aspect of our spiritual life. But what struck us is how rarely in those same small groups, Bible studies, and Sunday school classes we talk about our *experience with God!*

That is surprising, confounding, and sad for all of us in the mainline denominations, and perhaps especially so for those of us who are United Methodist. Because, as United Methodists, we have a Wesleyan heritage that is rooted in the practices of John and Charles Wesley and Francis Asbury. We are children of the Aldersgate experience. John Wesley found his heart to be "strangely warmed" as he came to an assurance of his faith in Jesus Christ. We are to be people not only of the clear head but also the warm heart—to be people who share not only our understanding of God but also our experience with God.

The early Methodists knew and practiced this consistently in their class meetings. In every meeting, they were asked the question of accountable discipleship, to which each member of the Wesleyan covenant class would answer: "How goes it with your soul?" The members of the class shared their personal experience with God and not just their understanding and thinking of God. We might ask the question this way: "How have you experienced God recently in your life?" How have you experienced God's forgiveness or grace or compassion in your life lately? Or, how have you experienced God's comfort or hope or support? Or, how have you experienced God's challenge or direction or will? The question is *not* about how you came to faith years ago, and it's not about the history of your church. It's about your real life and God's part in it, today.

How have you experienced God recently in your life?

The early Methodists shared their faith so widely with unconnected persons *because* they regularly shared their faith with other persons of faith in their class meetings. They had practiced sharing their faith. So if we are going to become persons who share our faith with those outside the church, we first have to become persons who regularly share our faith with persons inside the church.

We mainline Christians have lost our story. That's not to say we don't have a story. But we have simply lost the art of sharing our story with others. Many churches do baptism remembrance services on a regular basis. This is a way to remember your story of how God is experienced in your life. The Old Testament is full of remembering our story so that it could be passed on. This is not about church history, but the stories of our faith journey. So tell me about a time you have experienced God in your life lately. As Wesley asked, "How is it with your soul?"

We must find our own story.

There are at least three significant benefits from sharing your faith with other persons of faith in your small group. The first benefit of the sharing is nothing less than a potential reorientation of your whole life around the centrality of God's presence in your life. Let's describe simply how this happens. When you gather with your small group, you now know that every time you come you will be asked the question of accountable discipleship: "How have you experienced God recently in your life?" You know that question is coming when you attend a group; there is no surprise. You want to come prepared with your answer, as you don't want to look stupid when you are asked this key question. So during your week, you are consistently looking for how God is involved in your life, so that you will be able to answer that discipleship question when you gather with your small group. When you are continually looking for where God is in your life—guess what? You see God's presence and footprint all over your life! In other words, you see how deeply and consistently God is involved in your life. This means you see your life differently and more constantly oriented around that grace-filled presence of God. Stated negatively, if you are never asked about how you are experiencing

God, it is entirely possible to live your life from Sunday to Sunday without reference to or awareness of God, and become functional agnostic or atheist.

The second benefit of sharing your faith in your small group is the possibility of helping others deepen their faith in Jesus Christ or actually come to faith. When new people are invited to come to the group, they hear others share with each other how they have experienced God's presence in a real and personal way recently in their lives. The new people may not be aware of any such experience in their own lives, but perhaps they enjoyed the hospitality of the group and are intrigued by the possibility of God being present. They know the question of accountable discipleship is coming again next week, and so they began to look for God in their lives in the ways they've heard others in the group describe. When they start looking for where God is in their own life experience—guess what? They discover God's presence all over their lives. It is not surprising that, looking back, they would see God's work in their lives. We call that prevenient grace: God loving us before we were ever aware of it. And so our sharing of our faith in small groups can actually help others come to faith—and that is awesome!

The third benefit is that when we share our faith consistently in our small group—week in and week out, month in and month out—we are not only keeping God at the center of our own life experience and helping those unconnected discover God's presence in their own life. We are also regularly practicing to share our faith in Jesus Christ with others in our network of relationships. Faith sharing is not limited to a tract with four spiritual laws, pressing for a conversion. Faith sharing is simply sharing our experience of God in our lives and leaving the conversion work to the Holy Spirit.

Persons who actually practice this faith sharing make the following kinds of comments on their experience: "Bonding . . . Inspiring . . . Spiritually deepening . . . Fresh awareness of God in my life . . . Energizing . . . Uplifting . . . Supportive. . ." Imagine the difference it could make in your own spiritual life if you regularly shared your experience of God with others and

Practice your story in safe places.

heard their sharing as well. Imagine if this were not just a singular experience, but a regular event.

Not everybody has to be ready to share his or her experience of God with others in a group to begin this process. You can invite those who have regularly been involved in relational evangelism through service to participate in this faith sharing regularly in a group. Additionally, not every group that begins to have participants share their experience with God needs to be a new group. This faith sharing can become a part of an existing group. If the group is larger than five or six persons, this faith sharing can be done in threes or fours within the larger group. Not everybody has to hear everyone's faith story every time you meet. But everyone needs to share his or her experience with God and with others in the group each time you meet.

We would also note that sharing your experience with God in your small group is very appealing to children, youth, and younger adults (postmoderns). The key feature of effective ministry with postmoderns, described by Leonard Sweet in his book *Postmodern Pilgrims*, is that their encounter be experiential. Postmoderns don't just want to talk about what they think about God and what they understand about God. They also want to share their current experience with God. Faith sharing is consistent with postmodern ministry.

Take a few moments and think about how you might start to encourage persons in your church to share their experience of God with others. Whom would you invite to start this process? Which of your congregants are ready to take this step? What groups or classes do you believe would be ready to add this practice of faith sharing? What difference do you think this would make to the participants? What difference do you think this would make in the persons who begin to share experiences of God with others in the church? What difference do you think it would make in the life of your church to have a significant number of persons involved in sharing their experience of God with each other? What would it look like if we included this question: "Tell me about a time where you experienced God lately in your life"? What if this question were posed at the end of every choir practice, trustees' meeting, finance meeting, men's group, women's group, and ad board? What if this question were posed at your family dinner table routinely?

We have made an assumption that faith development occurs in the church. What we have learned is that real faith development begins at home and in our personal relationships with each other. Even as a United Methodist pastor, I (Bob) left the faith development of my children to the church, thinking that the church would take care of it and believing by my setting the example of going to church that they would get it. This is the assumption that parents in most mainline churches make and that my parents made. We thought we had it covered by taking our kids to youth group, Sunday school, VBS, and confirmation. Yet, when they graduated and went on with their lives, we realized that all we had given them was church. We didn't help them develop a personal experience/relationship in Jesus Christ.

We have practiced the very thing that John Wesley feared. His fear was that one day we would become the outer form of religion without the substance. We have good moral people who have good head knowledge. What they don't have is a life-giving, continually transforming personal experience with God. Kendra Creasy Dean explains this as Moralistic Therapeutic Deism (MTD) in *Almost Christian: What the Faith of Our Teenagers is Telling the American Church* (New York: Oxford, 2010, p. 14). This has led to a very shallow faith. It has left multiple generations wanting a more personal and real relationship with Jesus Christ as opposed to just playing church. So this tells us that faith development needs to start back at home. What would it look like if this began in our homes? The way to get back to a relationship with Christ is by getting back to the question of where God is at work in our lives. When we recognize where God is at work, we will have the stories to share.

As a layperson and a fourth-generation Methodist, I (Kay) have had a lifetime filled with "Methodist head knowledge." My mother took me to church and Sunday school when I was very young. I was certainly taught moral values in my home. But as my older sisters became teenagers and had other options for how to spend their Sundays, our family's church attendance began to be erratic. Before long, we became "C&E" (Christmas & Easter) attenders. So in my junior and senior high school days, church was pretty non-existent. This was especially true when the youth group at my small-town church collapsed. Being raised in the church gave my mother the reassurance that she had done all she needed to do to ensure I had the proper religious foundation.

As an adult and now a parent myself, I have come to realize that I was never taught, nor did I even recognize the lack of, a personal relationship with Christ in my life until I was well into my twenties. We never did talk about our faith at home. We went through the motions of going to church because that is "just what you are supposed to do." It was never about anything other than that—the outward appearance of being religious and doing the right thing. It wasn't until I joined a small group and people began to share their life struggles that I began to have a relationship with Jesus Christ. It is my prayer that my teenage son will develop that personal relationship with Christ through not only our regular

*worship attendance, his Sunday school attendance, and his deep connection to
our youth group, but also the conversations, questions, and modeling of both my*

Just playing church is no longer acceptable.

husband and me in our home.

Just playing church is no longer acceptable. Our faith must have deeper
roots than head knowledge and moral values. Our faith must be grounded in
a relationship with Jesus Christ that we regularly experience in a transforming, life-giving way and that we share with others.

After you have a significant number of persons in your church practicing sharing their faith in small groups for several months—congratulations!
You can continue to practice with competence and confidence Step One:
Relational evangelism through service and Step Two: Relational evangelism
through faith sharing. You are ready to move to Step Three: Sharing your faith
in worship. This is high school evangelism.

Chapter

FAITH SHARING IN WORSHIP

High school has many similarities to middle school. You still have a variety of teachers. You still travel to a variety of classrooms instead of staying in the same classroom. You still have classes with many different classmates. High school is still about identity, communication, and relationships, but going there requires taking the next steps in the advancement of learning and practice.

The same is true of high school evangelism. It takes us a little farther out of our comfort zone, but it builds on and deepens what we've already been practicing in the middle school evangelism of sharing experiences of God with others in our small group. We describe high school evangelism as sharing our faith in worship. This used to be referred to as sharing testimonies and was regularly practiced in worship at many churches. But often that faith sharing centered on the experience of coming to faith in Jesus Christ, rather than on the person's current experience. We want to focus on sharing our recent experience with God, for the edification of the persons with whom we are worshiping. This sharing in worship is similar to the sharing we experience in small groups. In other words, faith sharing in worship builds upon and is an extension of faith sharing in the small group.

Allow us to propose a couple of suggestions that we believe will help you avoid a potentially disastrous pitfall and will maximize the benefits that come with sharing faith in worship. We offer a strong word of caution: when you begin regularly having persons share their recent experience with God in worship, you may not want to do this like open mic night at the karaoke bar. In other words, you may not want to simply announce that anyone who would like to can step up on the spur of the moment and share their experience with God with those gathered for worship. This might be problematic; you do not want a person's sharing to result in inappropriate content in worship. Instead, allow your small groups to be the incubators for sharing in worship. When a person shares an experience of God in a small group and the group finds the story to be edifying, invite that person to share the same experience in worship.

You might find it very helpful to use digital recording as well as live sharing of faith experiences. There are several benefits that come with using digital recording. One is the capacity to edit for content and length. Another is the ability to include persons who are no longer able to attend worship (such as those who are homebound or in nursing facilities). What an amazing opportunity it is for these persons to share their faith experience with their church family, and in turn to remind the homebound faith-sharers that they are a vital part of the community of faith and that their faith journey is still important. Digital recording also enables those who are intimidated by public speaking to share their faith experience.

Another benefit of digital recording is the ability to time particular faith-sharing topics around sermon series, seasons, or particular worship themes. This also offers the opportunity to connect someone's experience in relational evangelism through service (Step One) and sharing faith with others in small groups (Step Two) to sharing in public worship (Step Three). For example, let's use a mission trip experience in these three steps. I (Bob) witnessed numerous people who experienced life-changing events on their trip to Juarez, Mexico, building houses. Our task was to build houses. And we did. But the real result was not building houses, but loving people. The mission was building relationships with the people we were serving. The participants could talk of nothing else all the way home! They later would be asked to share their mission trip experience with people in a Sunday school class. People would be so moved with the sharing of their mission trip experience that they would then be asked to share in worship. This sharing compels others in the congregation to go on a mission trip.

Here is another example of using a faith-sharing experience in worship. At Church of the Shepherd, my staff and I (Bob) were working on helping our congregation become regular givers and move into tithing. We knew that electronic fund transfer (EFT) is a great tool to help our congregation accomplish this easily. Our first attempt in getting people to sign up for EFT failed miserably. In trying to determine a better strategy, the administrative board decided to model the behavior by practicing it themselves. At the end of the first year, a person on the board had tithed for the first time. The person began to talk about how participation in the EFT process had been life changing. The money was subtracted from a bank account routinely and automatically. The person didn't have to think about it or remember to write a check. At the end of the year, the tithe had occurred without any disruption in the person's lifestyle whatsoever. That person's life had changed because of that first tithing experience and the joy felt in being able to accomplish it.

Faith sharing starts with leaders.

That person shared this life-changing experience with others in a small group (the administrative board), and it touched the others serving on the board. Those on the board felt the story would speak to others on a wider scale in worship. As a result of that faith sharing in worship, 43 percent of the budget of Church of the Shepherd now comes from EFT, ten years later. People respond to others' lives being changed. The act of participating in automatic EFT for the sake of the tithe meant nothing until it was tied to a personal story of how the simple choice of signing up for EFT changed a person's life.

Offer a consistent faith-sharing story during worship. I (Bob) would ensure we shared a two-minute video of a faith story. At the conclusion of the video, I would tie the faith story into the offering. I would point out that the offering makes our faith sharing and other missions possible, and I would thank the congregation for their giving. Then I would then ask them to give some more. Offerings went up each and every time we did this at Church of the Shepherd. Find a faith story to share on a monthly basis that somehow ties into the generosity of your congregation. My prayer before the offering is simply, "God, help us to be generous." Again, offerings always went up when we did this.

Offer consistent faith-sharing stories during worship.

This practice of faith sharing in worship is rooted in our Wesleyan experience. John and Charles Wesley regularly had laypersons share their faith as they conducted worship with field preaching. The Wesleys knew that a layperson sharing a personal experience with God had a tremendous impact and influence on those listening, especially those seeking in their relationship with God. Preaching was still important, but faith sharing was also an important component of the worship experience.

Faith sharing in worship is also consistent with postmodern worship. Leonard Sweet reminds us in *The Church of the Perfect Storm* that effective postmodern ministry is not only experiential, but also participatory. So when persons share their recent experience of God with others in worship, not only is it centrally experiential, but it also allows people to participate in worship through their sharing of their faith experience.

We want to invite you now to reflect on the possibility of faith sharing in worship at the church that you are a part of. Begin to think about how this could be implemented in your own context. Are there persons you can identify whom you could invite to share their experience of God with others in worship? What groups in your church have been practicing faith sharing and could be ready to recommend persons to share their faith stories in worship? How often might you include faith sharing in your worship experience? It need not be weekly, but could it be once or twice a month? At what point during the worship experience would you have faith sharing in worship occur? What difference do you believe regular faith sharing would make in the worship experience? What difference might this make for the worshipers? What difference might this make in the life of the congregation?

Ah, you already know what's coming—congratulations! You have now been practicing relational evangelism through service (Step One). You have been practicing faith sharing with people you already know at church in small groups (Step Two). You have shared your testimony in worship (Step Three). After a significant number of people have practiced all three steps regularly over several months, you are now ready to add the practice of college evangelism (Step Four): inviting others you do not know to worship.

FAITH SHARING
WITH THE UNCONNECTED

In the final stage of our school analogy, we are ready to tackle college evangelism. We have learned elementary evangelism: relational evangelism through service. We have learned middle school evangelism: faith sharing in a small group. The last chapter took us to high school evangelism: faith sharing in worship. It is now time for Step Four: inviting others to attend worship.

To be ready for college, preparation in high school is required. The practices of high school are developed, deepened, and expanded during the college experience. By the same token, faith sharing in small groups and in worship leads to inviting people to worship. Now some of you might take issue with this notion. You might reason that inviting someone to worship is not as challenging as sharing our recent experience with God in our small group or in worship. Therefore, inviting others to worship God would be more like middle school evangelism, which would be followed by the high school evangelism of sharing our experience of God in our small group, which would then be followed by the college evangelism of sharing our faith in worship. So why place inviting others to worship at this later point in the process of developing persons in the congregation to practice evangelism?

Allow us to explain our reasoning with an example from one denomination that we contend holds true for most mainline churches. Did you know that the average United Methodist member invites someone to come to worship once every thirty-eight years? Really. Once every thirty-eight years?

Unfortunately, it's true. Why do mainline church members so very infrequently invite others to worship? One reason is that we often mistake a wish for an invitation. We tell someone, "I'd like for you to come to worship some time at my church." But this is not an invitation—it is simply a wish, with little chance of being fulfilled. **An invitation has three characteristics:**

1. It is **personal** (phone to phone, face to face, or Facebook to Facebook).

2. It is **specific** ("I want to invite you to come on May 13 at 10 o'clock for worship and lunch afterward").

3. It is **relational** ("I want to invite you to come with me to worship on May 13. Would you like for me to pick you up?").

The second important reason why people so infrequently invite others to worship is that they are deeply afraid of the question they might be asked in response to their invitation. Let's say you invite your good friend Terry, whom you socialize with regularly, to come with you to worship on May 13. In response comes the question that you have been dreading might occur: "Thanks for inviting me to come with you to worship. But WHY should I come with you to worship? Why do you go to worship?" You proceed to stumble, fumble around, and realize you have no response. Why? Because you haven't first been practicing middle school evangelism, which is sharing your recent experience of God in your small group. If you had been doing that regularly before you invited Terry to worship, Terry's question would have posed no significant problem. The answer to that question is similar to the question of accountable discipleship you would have been regularly answering in your small group: "How have you experienced God recently in your life?" Your answer to Terry's question might go like this: "Why do I go to worship? I go to worship to celebrate God's love, which is an ongoing part of my life. For example, just last week I experienced God in my life this way." Your sharing of your faith in your small group would have prepared you to answer Terry's question. Regularly sharing your faith in your small group provides you the competence and confidence to share your faith and to answer other people's honest questions about why you go to church. If you practice sharing your faith in your small group, you are much more likely to invite someone else to come to worship with you.

There are other reasons that people are afraid or lack confidence to invite others to attend worship. They might worry about bad preaching or poor worship, music, or hospitality. It might be due to a previous bad experience with visitors. People are not willing to risk their weekday relationships on the possibility of their guest having a bad experience in worship. Most mainline church people have had that bad experience and won't risk it again. This is why we must build a culture of hospitality and passionate worship, so that people have the confidence to invite people to worship. We will address how to build this culture of hospitality in Section Three.

Special Sundays give people a reason to invite.

We recommend a particular process for inviting people to worship. This process was developed by Joe Harding during his tenure as lead pastor of Central Protestant Church in Richland, Washington, and has worked for more than thirty years. Joe later became the head of the Board of Evangelism for the United Methodist Church due in large part to the effectiveness of his ministry in his local church. His simple process for inviting others to worship can be used consistently in other churches as well.

Harding's process begins four weeks before "Invitation Sunday." On the first Sunday in worship, each worship folder (bulletin or program) contains a blank index card. During the prayer time in the worship service, all are encouraged to consider their own network of personal relationships and then to write on their index card the names of up to three persons who are not connected to any church. After the names are written on the index cards, the pastor invites each worshiper to pray for the welfare of each of the three people and for the opportunity to invite them to come to worship. All are then encouraged to take their prayer cards home and put them where they will see them every day (refrigerator, shaving mirror, makeup mirror) and pray for the welfare of each person on their cards and for the opportunity to invite them to come to worship.

The next Sunday (three weeks before Invitation Sunday), during the prayer time, the pastor encourages anyone who has not filled out their index card to do so and then asks a key accountability question. (As we learned from John Wesley, effective ministry requires consistent support and clear accountability.) The pastor asks for everyone who has regularly been praying for the persons on their prayer cards to raise their hands. Now we realize that some persons will put their hands in the air as a prayer of confession ("Lord, I'm sorry that I forgot to pray for the persons on my card. Please forgive me.

I promise I'll do better.") But for most, it is a way of providing accountability to follow through on the prayer card with the invitation.

The next Sunday (two weeks before Invitation Sunday), during the prayer time, the pastor asks two questions of accountability. First, raise your hand if you have been praying for the persons on your prayer card. Second, raise your hand if you have invited them to come with you to worship. You can see that each week the accountability is repeated and expanded.

The last Sunday (the week before Invitation Sunday), during the prayer time, the pastor asks three questions of accountability. First, raise your hand if you have been praying for the persons on your prayer card. Second, raise your hand if you have invited them to come with you to worship. Third, raise your hand if you know they are coming. If you don't know if they're coming, this week is a great opportunity to follow up with your invitation.

Central Protestant Church used this process regularly two to three times a year for more than fourteen years. The church consistently saw an increase in worship attendance of more than 50 percent on Invitation Sundays. As a result of those invitations, the church grew in average worship attendance from about three hundred and fifty to more than twelve hundred during that fourteen-year span. People will not come until we first go. And invitation is one of the most effective ways for us to go and for them to come. Strategically, it is best to hold Invitation Sundays before Christmas, before Easter, and before back-to-school. In Section Three, you will be introduced to another example of how to invite people to worship after a church bridge event.

Invitation is also consistent with postmodern ministry. Adam Hamilton, lead pastor of the Church of the Resurrection in Leawood, Kansas, shared this observation in his workshop at the Leadership Institute. At his church, young adults tend to respond more positively to an invitation to come first to a service project, followed by an invitation to worship or to visit a small group. In other words, we can invite people to help us serve in our relational evangelism through service (Step One or elementary school evangelism), to attend our small groups (Step Two or middle school evangelism), and to worship (Step Three or high school evangelism). Postmoderns respond well to invitation, rather than simply information.

Relationship comes before invitation.

Remember, an invitation comes best after you build a relationship. Otherwise, it is an empty invitation. How do you do that? That's what is next in Section Two!

Take time to reflect on this process of invitation. How could you use this in your church? Whom could you invite to worship within the next month? What difference would it make if you regularly had Invitation Sundays as a part of the evangelism of your church? What difference would it make in your own spiritual life to regularly invite others to come with you to worship, to your small group, and to serve?

And so—congratulations! You are ready now to enter into graduate school evangelism. You're ready to learn how to develop relationships, listen to the faith journey of another person, enter into conversations where you share your experience of God with the other person, and help that person move toward a significant relationship as a growing disciple of Jesus Christ.

BECOME A TWENTY-FIRST CENTURY MISSIONARY

The word *evangelism* simply scares mainline people. It may well be the most dreaded ten-letter word in the Christian vocabulary! This is true for both laity and clergy. We sometimes try to talk about it and tiptoe around the subject, trying not to even use the "E" word. The word itself may put people off. There have been some evangelists who have scared us into thinking we must Bible thump on the street corner and yell at people in order to be an evangelist.

We have done a poor job of creating a positive picture of what it means to be an evangelist or what it means to be a missionary in America. We may use *evangelist* and *missionary* interchangeably, but no matter what we say here, "goofy" ideas will come into our heads. And we may immediately jump to the conclusion that we are not evangelists, nor do we ever intend to become evangelists. Would it be easier to imagine that our everyday lifestyles could encompass the idea of being a missionary? Could we imagine taking our everyday lives and seeing them as opportunities to be about the missional work of Jesus Christ? Can my life become missional? Being missional seems to be less frightening. But without an intentional plan of becoming missional, we risk living our lives as secularly as those who have never experienced God.

The aim of this section is to take the mystery and discomfort out of the process of becoming more missional. (Remember, *missional* does mean evangelistic, but we will continue to use *missional* to keep the stress at bay!) We will lift up some strategies that can allow evangelism to be a part of your everyday life. Evangelism isn't just something for the pastor or the few brave souls who dare to join the evangelism committee at the church. Our aim is to move evangelism from abstract theory into action in your everyday life, whether you are laity or clergy. Just a quick warning: this may seem a bit out of your mainline comfort zone in the beginning. But it will become easier as we venture into the material.

In Chapter Five, we will share practical ideas about starting conversations with people we don't know without being obnoxious. In Chapter Six, we will share how to create opportunities for new relationships in your natural settings. In Chapter Seven, we will share how to move mere acquaintances to authentic relationships. Those relationships might give us the chance to have a faith conversation with someone, and that conversation might lead them into community with Jesus Christ.

In our Healthy Church Initiative consultation, loyal church members often come to us with these questions: Isn't it enough just to live my life as a good example? Isn't it enough to live a good, clean moral life? Isn't it enough to do the good deeds? Isn't it enough to let my example speak for itself? What gives us the right to impose our understanding of God on someone else? I don't want people to think I am "wacko" or "weird." I am turned off by that stuff, so others will certainly be turned off as well. Isn't evangelism about the numbers anyway?

Every church has two mission fields.

We have two mission fields. The first is to deepen the connected people we already know in their love of God and their love for one another in our church. If we don't care for this first mission field properly, it will stop us from reaching the second mission field. And yet, if all we do is take care of the first mission field and we miss the second mission field, the church becomes inwardly focused and dies a very slow, painful death. This second mission field is to take God's love to the people we don't already know and who are not already Christians (the unconnected). The primary aim of this book is to help us with mission field number two. This is because every time we raise the flag to take care of ourselves, we must raise the flag nine times to remind us to take care of someone else. Our natural state as humans is to take care of ourselves first. The same is true of our churches. But when we don't also address the second mission field, our churches die.

The prophets Jeremiah and Ezekiel condemned the shepherds for failing to take care of mission field one and field two. It wasn't one or the other. It must consistently be both (Ezekiel 34:1–6). When we look at the life of Jesus Christ, he didn't just let his life speak for itself. He engaged in conversations and relationships both inside and outside the church. The fact is, he was continuously confronting the religious leaders of his day because they were upset with him for spending time with people they didn't know (the unconnected). The heart of Jesus and his ministry is summarized in Mathew 9:18–38.

God desperately loves us, and God desperately loves the rest of world. God needs us to demonstrate that love to the world. It is simply not enough to clothe the poor; we need the spirit as well (Matthew 5:13–16). We are not to worry about what the moths eat on the outside, but we are to be concerned about what is on the inside. Throughout the New Testament, Christ tells us to combine the good deeds with the good words. Jesus Christ, the Scriptures, the church, and the disciples all reveal the need to hang out with people we do not know (the unconnected) and nurture them into a relationship with Christ so that they can know the truth of life.

Why count?

Now let's discuss numbers. We find it interesting that there is such a strongly adverse reaction to the concept of *counting*. Yet Jesus counted time after time. He counted how many came for the fishes and loaves on the hillside. He counted the number of baskets, both the number they started with and the number they ended with. In the Acts New Testament church, they counted at least three times: at the beginning, in the middle, and at the end. Jesus cared about numbers because he cared deeply about results and people. In Matthew 7:16, he says, "You will know them by their fruit" (ISV). Jesus came across a fig tree that bore no fruit and, being unmoved by the natural explanations (that is, that it was out of season), he withered the fig tree anyway.

Bishop William H. Willimon, in *Bishop: The Art of Questioning Authority by an Authority in Question*, states: "In North Alabama we define clergy effectiveness in one biblically based word: growth. Effective pastors know how to lead growth. Lists of nice-to-have qualities (π 304: Qualifications for Ordination, Book of the Discipline) are useless and therefore un-Wesleyan. A pastor who grows things is effective: a pastor who knows only how to lead shrinkage is ineffective" (p. 52).

There is a balance here between always counting for the sake of numbers and never counting for any sake. It is true that numbers do not tell the whole story. It is also true that prior to any numbers, there are always describe-ables. Describe-ables are ministries that change lives. Someone has experienced God. Transformation has taken place. But the truth is that when a describe-able event occurs, it almost always results in something measurable. We also contend that if ministries are not adding growth to your congregation, then something else is wrong. It is like a young child who is growing smarter all the time. Even though the child is growing, the doctor wants to obtain measurements such as height, weight, pulse, blood pressure, and blood count to prove the child's health. Measurables and describe-ables go together. If you have only describe-ables and no measurables, something is wrong. If all you have are measurables and no describe-ables, then something is wrong.

Let's begin this journey for a new way of thinking about becoming missional.

BEGINNING OUTSIDE CONVERSATIONS

In 1987, I (Bob) went to India on a mission interpretation team so that I could come back to America to raise money for wells, medical clinics, and churches. Having never been to India before, I contemplated what clothes I would need to pack, what food I would eat while I was there, who I would be with on the trip, what worship would be like there, how to use the transportation system, what I might do and experience while visiting, and so on. Interestingly enough, none of my preconceived ideas about India ended up being true. My assumptions were all wrong because I didn't know the culture. None of my clothes matched the culture. The food was unexpected. The experiences and people I encountered were not what I expected. Nothing that I prepared for in my brain matched the reality in India.

This is exactly what the church is faced with today. We, the church in America, used to exist at the center of culture. In other words, we lived in a church-centric world. Today, we are in a secular world where the church no longer plays the central role. Yet we are still making assumptions about what the people need and want as though we are still living in a church-centric world. On my trip to India, I didn't have to adapt to the Indian culture. I was leaving in three weeks, so I didn't need to learn the local ways. I was a visitor. If I were to live in India, I would have to adapt to the culture. This would include changes in my language, clothing, worship, relationships, housing, and more. Churches of today live in a foreign land with a foreign culture.

But we have not adapted to this new land where we find ourselves living. We keep thinking people should come to us. We think people should act like us. We think people should like what we like. At best, we are pretending that we are visiting a foreign land but don't intend to stay. We are as far away from understanding the culture in our churches today as I was to understanding the culture during my trip to India.

Our defenses rise when we encounter this new culture. The church is supposed to be a refuge and a fortress! The song "A Mighty Fortress is Our God" comes to mind. Yet wasn't it Jesus who challenged us to live in the world but not of the world?

> "I am coming to you now, but I say these things while I am still in the world, so that they may have the full measure of my joy within them. I have given them your word and the world has hated them, for they are not of the world any more than I am of the world. My prayer is not that you take them out of the world but that you protect them from the evil one. They are not of the world, even as I am not of it. Sanctify them by the truth; your word is truth. As you sent me into the world; I have sent them into the world. For them I sanctify myself, that they too may be truly sanctified." John 17:13–19 (NIV)

Even the Pharisees were always chastising Jesus for being too much of the world and not enough in the church world.

Methodism swept across America in the late 1700s and early 1800s under the leadership of Francis Asbury. John Wigger writes in *American Saint Francis Asbury & The Methodists* that Francis Asbury was "the people's saint, an ordinary person who chose to do extraordinary things" (Oxford: Oxford University Press, 4). Wigger writes Asbury communicated his vision for Methodism in four enduring ways that came to define much of evangelical culture in America.

1. The first was through his legendary piety and perseverance, rooted in a classically evangelical conversion experience.

2. The second way that Asbury communicated his vision was through his ability to connect with ordinary people.

3. The third conduit of Asbury's vision was the way that he understood and used popular culture. Henry Rack argues persuasively that Wesley acted as a "cultural middleman" between Methodists on the one hand and clergymen and educated gentlemen in England on the other.

4. The fourth way that Asbury communicated his message was through his organization of the Methodist church. He was a brilliant administrator and a keen judge of human motivations.

Like Asbury, we need to become the modern-day or twenty-first century missionaries. If we are going to engage the unconnected today, we must first be willing to learn the new world we are in and not kid ourselves that we are just visiting. We are simply not adapting to the culture in which we live today. We haven't learned the language. We don't understand people's likes and dislikes. We have not accepted their clothing, lifestyles, thinking, or worldview. The church has become the one place that doesn't have to change—the one and only place in our ever-changing lives that will remain unchanged. With a status quo church culture comes an inevitable decline in worship attendance. With that decline comes stress. Or if by chance there is change, then there is conflict over the loss of our church as the one constant, unchanging thing in our lives—our safe haven.

The church has become a generational entity. We have passed our church down from one generation to the next. We have not reached outside our own families. This became obvious at our Healthy Church Initiative consultation weekends. The Healthy Church Initiative is a process created in the Missouri Annual Conference of the UMC under the leadership of Bob Farr. The process includes leadership development, accountability, coaching, laity involvement, and on-site church consultations. During the consultation, we would ask participants a series of questions about how they came to that particular congregation:

- Question One: *How did you become a United Methodist?* We found that most people became Methodist for one of two reasons. The predominant pathway is being born into the church. The second pathway is to marry into the church (spouse was already a Methodist).

- Question Two: *How did you come to this particular United Methodist Church?* People usually arrived via one of two routes. Most often, they found the church on their own: "I moved to town and looked up the local church like I'm supposed to, because I was already United Methodist or mainline Protestant." The second route of arrival was "I grew up here." Rarely did people report that they came via an invitation from another.

- Question Three: *Were you a Christian before you came to this church?* The overwhelming majority said yes.

This system of getting to the church worked when we were a church-centric culture. Over the past hundred years, we developed a system for affiliate members (people who were already Christians). We did not teach our pastors or laity how to compete for unconnected people's hearts and minds in a secular culture. This brings us to the obvious conclusion that we are too out of touch and out of practice to reach people. We are going to have to think more like Francis Asbury and less like our grandparents if we are to reach people for Jesus Christ.

There is also another confusing situation in mainline Christianity. When young people who are raised in the church go away from the church and then do come back, they tend to like things just the way they were. This is their expectation of church because it is the only thing they've ever known. It is their comfort zone. But it may not be the comfort zone of or relevant to most Millennials, who grew up outside the church. We found in our Healthy Church Initiative consultations that 90 percent of our youth graduate from church at confirmation and have never returned. This makes it incredibly difficult to figure out what the church must be doing to reach younger people.

The church has become an alien in our own world. We have to accept the fact that we are no longer just visiting like I (Bob) was in India. We are in this new culture for life. We must learn the new language, culture, and church systems. We will have to relearn much of what we are used to, in order to adapt to the local culture. This learning a new culture will be stressful for both our laity and clergy—especially because we have never practiced reaching people we do not already know. We are more than happy to receive people (both connected and unconnected) if they accept our preferences and likes. So we have not seen it as our obligation to change anything on the inside of the church, let alone have conversations with people we don't know outside the church.

On my (Bob's) India trip, our guide got us through by speaking the local language, knowing the terrain, and navigating the border crossings. The rest of us in the group didn't have to worry about any of those details. That works well for a short trip. But if I am staying for life, I can't rely on a guide or any single person to do that work for me. I have to do it myself. I have to adapt. I have to think differently if I am to thrive.

Adapting does not mean we are giving up our values or our experiences of God. But we are going to have to sacrifice some of our preferences and likes in order to reach unconnected people with different preferences and likes. We believe that is precisely where the church is today. We have to learn to reach people we don't know in a culture we do not understand.

So how do we begin conversations with people we do not know? It begins as seeing every human interaction as an opportunity to have a genuine conversation. We recognize that 90 percent of the time we miss the opportunity. Only 10 percent of the time do we catch the signal that a conversation is possible. But if we are not looking or thinking beyond ourselves, we will never start any conversation. We will miss the opportunity each and every time. Start looking around! The precursor to Step One is to engage the radar antenna. Do you remember Radar (Walter) O'Reilly in the 1970s hit *M.A.S.H.*? He had an innate ability to know what people were going to say before they ever said it. He had a "radar." Do you have a radar? In the rest of this chapter, we will begin to train ourselves to engage in our opportunities. Imagine the opportunities we have missed because our radar was not engaged. Engage the radar!

Engage the radar!

CONVERSATION STARTER STORY

I (Bob) was in Tampa, Florida, in a bar and grill packed with people during lunch, sitting with six of my colleagues at a table in the middle of the restaurant. I intentionally sat at the end of the table to allow for more of a chance to talk to other tables and waitresses. We were really involved in our own conversation and not paying much attention to those around us. At the tail end of lunch, I turned around and spotted a guy with a Harley t-shirt sitting at the table next to me. I asked if he rode. He said he did. I shared with him that I was a new rider. We discussed the specifics and showed each other pictures of our bikes. I had traded my vintage Mustang for my Harley. This led to our shared stories of Mustangs. The man then asked me where I was from. I told him I was from St. Louis, Missouri. He then asked why I was in Tampa, Florida. I told him I was a United Methodist pastor in town for a conference. The man laughed and then said he had never met a pastor before who owned a Harley. He said that if he were to go church, he wanted to go to the kind of church where the pastor rode a Harley.

This is an example of watching for opportunities. If I were from Tampa, Florida, I would have handed him my card and invited him to my church. My colleagues at lunch did not have their radar antennae up. We were all inwardly focused on our own conversation—so much so that I almost missed the opportunity to start the conversation with the man in the Harley t-shirt.

Too often, we are inwardly focused on our own conversations, desires, and concerns, not paying any attention to the world around us and therefore not starting the conversation and not changing any lives.

Our goal is to encourage you to start a conversation once a day with someone you don't know so that it might lead to a faith story. Here are the steps to allow this to happen:

STEP ONE: HAVE AN INTENTIONAL PLAN

Without this goal and intentional plan, you will not be looking for opportunities. When starting my (Bob's) new church in 1990, it was imperative that I learn to start conversations with people I did not know, because I had no one inside the church. I had to figure this out and make it a part of my everyday living in my ordinary life without being obnoxious. How do you find those opportunities? Where could you look for affinities and commonalities with other people outside your church? These shared interests allow the opportunity for conversation starters. When our radar is engaged, we are looking for commonalities with people around us.

In the Tampa restaurant, the commonality was the Harley t-shirt. I (Bob) ride a Harley. I like to hear and share stories about Harleys. It was a safe way in which to begin to engage with someone, because we shared common ground.

Another commonality is the fire service. I (Bob) am a volunteer firefighter. Police are also a commonality for me, as my dad was a volunteer deputy sheriff. What are your commonalities? Where do you hang out? What do you like to do or experience in your leisure time? God works best through the things you are already interested in. What gives the "E" word a bad name is that we are convinced we have to do things we don't like, in places we don't like, saying things we don't like with people we don't know. But God works best through our natural setting. Those places where we are most comfortable.

Doug hung out at the basketball court and the Little League diamond. Kay is not going to hang out in fire stations. One of the places she likes to go is to the movies.

God works best through our natural settings.

I (Kay) grew up never having thought about the possibility of having a radar, let alone engaging my radar. But as my faith has grown, I am now aware I have a radar and try to engage it intentionally. It is simply amazing how many opportunities present themselves when we are open and looking for them. Just the other day, I was attending a movie at my local theater with an out-of-town guest. I had been having trouble with my frequent guest card and decided to stop at Guest Services to see if I could clear up the issue. The young man present tried to take care of the issue without much luck. Another young man appeared and began trying to solve the issue using a different method.

In the meantime, another guest with a similar problem came onto the scene. Because there was only one computer, the two employees were able to address only one issue at a time. Even before the two young men were able to start addressing the other guest's issue, the other guest started bad-mouthing the system, theater, and program. She was impatient and belligerent. Both young men kept apologizing to both of us for the delay and were doing their best to handle the situation. The other woman just kept spewing ugly remarks, and I could see the young men were becoming anxious. It was then that I said, "It is obvious that this woman's problem is much more critical and urgent than mine. I will come back another time." Both young men looked at me and were surprised by my statement. I assured them it was okay, and they both thanked me for my patience and apologized for not being able to correct the problem. I then watched the movie with my friend.

As we exited the theater, one of the young men from Guest Services flagged me down. He asked me to accompany him to the Guest Services desk. He proceeded to tell me that he was so appreciative of my patience and my allowing them to service the other guest that he wanted to give me two movie passes and correct the issue on my frequent guest card. I told him that he didn't need to do that, but I appreciated his kindness just the same. He said he wanted to tell me that he had never seen anyone act as I did and that it meant very much to him. I told him I just tried to practice being kind to other people as a part of my lifestyle. I have been back to that theater again since this happened, and we now know each other's names. I will continue to pursue a friendly conversation with him each time I go to the movies, with the hope that one day it will turn into an opportunity to share my faith story.

You can't be afraid to follow conversations started by others, too. A waitress, for example, once commented when she left the ticket that the people at my (Bob's) table were sure having a good time and were being loud. She asked why. I responded that we were United Methodist! It opened up the conversation, and we discussed being United Methodist, being a pastor, and the question of whether she had a church home. The local church pastor I was with then had the perfect opportunity to introduce himself and offer his card and an invitation. My radar was up!

We want to get to the point where our radar is always engaged naturally, when it becomes a part of who we are and how we go about life. Being missional is a way of life. It is not just a trip, a check, or donating a can of green beans. But before it becomes woven into who we are and how we operate, we must first be aware, be intentional, work a plan, assess how we are doing, and make adjustments to our approaches. Every approach will be different. Remember, this is more of an art than a science.

> **Evangelism is more of an art than a science.**

STEP TWO: SET A DAILY GOAL

Set a daily goal of how many opportunities you will find to start conversations. An insurance salesman once told me (Bob) that each time he started a conversation with someone he didn't know, he moved something from his right to his left pocket to note that one of his ten contacts for the day had been met. I decided that I would try this. I inherited marbles from my great-grandmother Clara Farr, a preacher's kid whose father was a circuit rider in Missouri in the late 1800s in the Dunkards Church. (Dunkards were forerunners of the Brethren Church and the Disciples of Christ Church in Missouri.) Grandma Clara received the marbles from her father. Of course, after I decided to try the salesman's conversation-counting technique, I instantly thought of the ten marbles that Great-Grandma Clara gave to me. Each time I started a conversation with someone I didn't know, I moved one of those marbles from my right pocket to my left pocket. I didn't allow myself to end the day until all ten marbles were in my left pocket. I repeated this day after day for three years. This reminded me to be a missionary. This is how I started Grace Church UMC, Lee's Summit, Missouri.

If you don't set a goal to start conversations, then it is not going to happen. What can you do in your personal life to set a similar goal and accomplish it? Being a follower of Christ takes much self-discipline. Practice! The more we do it, the more comfortable we become with the process and the more effective we will become. The more we do it, the more it will also become a natural process.

STEP THREE: BUILD TRUST

Trusting that God is building a real relationship with somebody is the most important thing. It usually goes well, and, simply, it doesn't go badly. There are certainly stories where it didn't go anywhere, but it doesn't go badly. We tend to shy away from the practice of the "E" word because we are fearful that it will turn bad. But we must trust that God is taking this conversation somewhere. We are not selling the church. We are not selling God. We are not selling Jesus. When we are trying to sell something, we may have bad experiences when we push toward our own ends. We don't like people trying to sell us something in a pushy way. Most of us have had religious people being pushy, trying to sell their church. This is not a selling process. This is a relationship-building process. Trust that prevenient grace will prevail. Don't be scared of it! Be yourself! Don't be somebody else. Be open to have the natural conversation that might lead to a natural faith conversation. This is why it is important to work through your connections and affinities in your natural hang-out places. You just need to be you with your radar engaged. We are not asking you to be Billy Graham! Be you!

> **Remember: This is not about selling.**

Think about how Jesus went about this. Jesus started a casual conversation at the well asking about water. And he let the woman at the well lead the conversation. Remember how Jesus met Zacchaeus? He met him in a tree. He didn't want to go to church with him. He wanted to go to his house for dinner. Think of how Jesus found his disciples along the seashore among fishermen. He started the conversation not about religious topics but by asking if they would like to catch some fish. Jesus' example teaches us to hang out in places that are not religious to converse with people who are not religious (the unconnected). So put your radar up and trust that God will take the conversation in the right direction.

STEP FOUR: MUTUAL RESPECT

We believe the reason conversations have not gone bad is because we have mutual respect for others. We are not trying to bring them to salvation in this initial conversation. We are not being obnoxious about our beliefs. We are just trying to be authentic and show interest in others. We think people have a true desire for conversation and connection. Starbucks is not really about selling coffee. It is more about creating an atmosphere for people to have conversations. People at Starbucks may seem to be engrossed in their iPads or laptops, but they are most likely looking for relationships. Think about it. People could do Facebook and Twitter from home with a free cup of coffee. People are open to the opportunity of having a conversation, especially when you show interest in who they are and what they like.

Despite all the modern day digital connection options, many psychologists find many people still suffer from isolation and loneliness. So just start a conversation! Remember, you are engaging in a conversation from a sincere interest in the other person, as opposed to starting with the three laws of salvation, or here's a Bible, or let me tell you about my beliefs. Remember, people need to belong before they believe. People need to feel connected before they engage. You are starting on common ground with mutual respect. Create an atmosphere that is comfortable for both the initiator (you) and the receiver (them). It cannot be forced. You are living in a different world. It will be difficult, but we can't be afraid. We are learning that young people want mentors. They want relationships with older adults as long as that relationship is a mutual, trusting relationship, which means you need to put your judgment in your pocket. Give it a try!

STEP FIVE: THE CONVERSATION

First find a way to connect. Remember the Harley t-shirt story or the act of kindness Kay demonstrated at the movie theater? There are many ways to connect. Consider Facebook, the line at the grocery store, asking about a person's computer or other electronic gadget, or the team logo on someone's cap or t-shirt. These are all ways to connect with a person. Make sure to concentrate the conversation on the other person and his or her story. Be curious. Ask questions. Guard against telling your story too much, too soon, too fast. Be prepared with the next question. A good question is worth a million dollars here. Your goal is first to hear that person's story and then to let it lead him or her to being curious about your story. The goal is to move the conversation to a place that sparks curiosity about you from the other person. Who you are and what you do is a question from the other person, as opposed to something you push on him or her. They ask for your story. You don't just tell it.

This shift of moving from their story to your story is the most important shift. This is where the conversation can dry up. Remember, this is an art and not a science. You must sprinkle in a bit of your faith story. Don't be afraid to identify yourself as a lay leader from the church. This is the juncture at which the conversation can dwindle. Be at peace if it doesn't go further. Be at peace if it does! Don't push. It is also important to hang out in the same places routinely, because it gives you more opportunities a week from now to continue the conversation. Remember, you are trying to build an authentic relationship here. You are not just seeking a conversion. You are looking for the conversation to mature over time. As the conversation continues, you will eventually be able to share your elevator speech (faith story). You will learn more about this in Chapter Seven. To recap, the conversation has four elements: connection, focus on them, spark curiosity about you, and then sprinkle in your faith story. Remember to be authentic. Be real. You are trying to build an authentic relationship—not a conversion. We aren't just trying to be friendly. We are trying to become a friend.

STEP SIX: BECOME A MODEL

When you practice starting conversations with people, you become a model for others. Others will begin to watch and listen and be curious about how your conversations are going. It also gives you stories to share back at the church. It gives you stories to share in your small group settings, Bible studies, and Sunday School classes (middle school evangelism). It may give you testimonies to share in a worship setting (high school evangelism). Pastors, if you have not practiced starting conversations with people you don't know, you don't have any stories to tell. It is difficult to teach and preach about evangelism if all you have is the theology but not the practice of evangelism. If you start doing this, you will have stories of evangelism for your faith sharing in service, small groups, and worship.

We are *all* missionaries.

We have all sorts of reasons why we don't do this. One of the main reasons is that we believe someone else will do it. They were born to do it. It's their "job" to do it—not mine. This is what we pay the pastor to do and why we have an Evangelism Committee. So, how's that working for us? If everyone were inviting someone to church as often as you invite someone to church, how would your church be doing? If everyone started a conversation with a stranger as often as you do, how would we be doing? We are all called to share. We just have to learn to do it in a way that is comfortable both for us and for those we encounter. Friends, we are in a "new world" as disciples of Christ. We are in a world where people don't trust the church. People don't know much about Jesus. And we are not sure that they are going to like our message. A recent Gallup poll reported that 92 percent of Americans believe there is a God (gallup.com/poll/147887/Americans-Continue-Believe-God.aspx). They want to read the Bible. They want to be spiritual. They like Jesus. But they don't like the church in its current condition.

We can change our current condition. It is not the condition that we have always been in. We must adapt to this new culture with a new plan to share our faith, as outlined in the six steps in this chapter. If we truly want people to experience God in their lives, we are going to have to start slowly and help them experience authentic relationships with us. If we ourselves want to experience a deeper relationship with Christ, it will most likely occur when we are starting conversations with people we don't know with the hope of sharing our story. Perhaps the mainline church is so dry spiritually because we are out of practice starting conversations and sharing our faith with people we don't know. When we are attempting to share our faith with others, we have to reach down and find our faith. This leads to a vitality and deepening of our own faith and experience with Jesus Christ. Imagine what could happen if a quarter of our churches were to engage in this practice on a regular basis! It could actually lead to what Bill Hybels calls "Contagious Christianity." In the next chapter, we will look for ways to create opportunities for new conversations and relationship building.

CREATING OPPORTUNITIES FOR NEW RELATIONSHIPS

One of the biggest risks for every mainline Christian is in spending all of our time with those who are already Christian. We reward our pastors specifically for spending time with those who are already connected in the church. If, in fact, a pastor decides to spend significant time in the mission field, he or she will likely receive significant pushback from the congregation: "Why don't you care about us? Isn't it more important to take care of us first?"

It is also true in the life of the church that we tie up our church leaders in the business of the church so that they don't have time to spend out in the mission field. In a seminar, Rick Warren explains that the church is the only organization that does not exist for its own members. In other words, it is not about us! A paramount challenge is determining how to change how we spend our time, how we spend our resources, and how we structure the very life and nature of the church.

How much of your time in every week do you spend out in your community with people you don't know? This is a question we ask pastors in a Healthy Church Initiative consultation. We find that 90 to 100 percent of their time is spent caring for the members and caring for the church. In churches that are growing, the clergy and the laity spend at least 20 percent of their time not maintaining the church but instead being out in the mission field with the unconnected, serving people they do not know. This means intentionally putting ourselves in places to meet new people. Pastor and laity must hold themselves accountable for the results of their ministries to reach new people as well as the people already in the church. Paul Borden once said in a seminar that members of each church should take responsibility for a certain percentage of their mission field and hold themselves accountable for that specific number. Until they do so, it is unlikely they will reach people for Jesus Christ.

How much time are you spending with the unconnected?

It is critical for a church to create opportunities to reach new people through its ministries. We often prescribe a ministry audit to determine whether a church's current ministries are reaching people for Christ. If those ministries are not reaching new people (the unconnected), strategies must be put in place for this to occur.

Pastors must hold themselves accountable for results. Pastors must take the first step and model reaching people for Christ. The more often we reach new people, the more comfortable we become with being outwardly focused. In turn, pastors will equip others in the congregation to do the same. You can't talk or teach others about relational evangelism if you don't have the experiences with it and therefore have stories to share and model for others. We often do not have an intentional process to make it happen, nor have we equipped people to feel comfortable in doing so. And remember, pastors rarely were taught relational evangelism in their seminary training. It is imperative as a church body to create opportunities to build relationships with people we do not know, knowing this is not the natural state of affairs in our mainline churches. Perhaps we might think about a different system that would reward pastors and laity for growing a church with people we do not know (the unconnected), as opposed to rewarding pastors and laity for maintaining "peace in the valley" for the connected, allowing our churches to decline as we take care of the people we already know.

For a pastor to move into this model and be out in the community meeting new, unconnected people, there has to be buy-in and communication from the church and its leaders. Pastor, it is very important to get with your personnel team to talk about the need to be outside in the community. This must be done first. Otherwise, your congregation will think you are out playing or goofing off! To spend eight to ten hours a week out in the community meeting new people, you will have to decide what you will no longer do in the church. This means you must look at all the things you do in a typical week and begin to prioritize the importance and effectiveness of how that time is spent. What things are you, the pastor, doing that someone else could be doing instead? What things are you doing with your time that really bear no fruit or return on your time investment? What are some things you are doing that could be done more effectively or efficiently using a different method (perhaps upgraded technology of some sort)? Are you matching your gifts with how you spend your time? What is keeping you from spending those eight to ten hours out in the community meeting new people?

Most pastors and churches are calendar driven. Weeks and months go by without any intentional outcomes. We were just fulfilling the events on the calendar from the year before. We wonder why our church is in decline or not growing, but we just don't equate that to the time we are spending behind our desks. We get caught up in one emergency after another. Stephen Covey reminds us there is a distinction between urgent and important tasks. Pastors have a lot of "urgent" on their desks. Rarely have we sorted out what the "important" really is. Most pastors say that they are really busy. I have no doubt that they are. But are they busy with the right things, the important things?

> **Concentrate on the important rather than the urgent.**

In churches under 150 in average worship attendance, the priorities for a pastor are congregational care, quality worship and preaching, lay leadership development, and being the main missionary in the community. For churches over 150 in average worship attendance, the priorities are the same, in addition to building teams. Depending on the size of the congregation, however, these priorities will be accomplished using different means and people. For instance, a pastor never moves completely out of congregational care, but as the church grows, the pastor will need to equip others to help with the congregational care. As the church grows, there may be more staff to help with any one of the ministries, as opposed to the pastor doing the ministries by him or herself. As a church grows, systems and teams of people will have to be put into place to accomplish the ministries that were often singlehandedly accomplished by pastors and laity in churches of smaller size. The pastor is always the main face of the church in the mission field and the main missionary for the unconnected; this never changes. As the church grows past 100 in worship attendance, if new systems and teams are not put into place, it will diminish the pastor's ability to be outwardly focused in the community as a missionary. Ninety percent of all mainline Protestant churches do not grow past 100 in worship attendance because the pastor is too busy "running" the church. In our previous book, *Renovate or Die*, we talk about the differences between a pastor-led (more than 150 in worship) versus a pastor-centered (fewer than 150 in worship) church. Refer to this book for more information.

If a pastor were to spend eight hours a week outside the church and, likewise, if lay people were to spend time each week pursuing these intentional conversations, just imagine what could happen! Lay persons will need to assess what they will give up to focus on intentional conversations with the unconnected. Once we begin this practice, we become more comfortable with the process and thus are more effective with it, until it becomes woven into our everyday lives. It becomes a habit and a way of life. It becomes a natural part of our interactions with people. As Wesley says, "We are a way of life."

People often say that everyone they know is already a Christian. We used to believe this was not true. But the more work we do in churches, the more we find this is actually true. Our churches have become social circles in and of themselves. We have formed such strong social bonds inside the church that we rarely have social circles outside the church. We have unintentionally become inwardly focused. Churches do not decide one day to become inwardly focused. They become inwardly focused over time. We must break this cycle in order to open ourselves up to opportunities to meet unconnected people. How do we break this cycle and get outside our normal patterns? We need to spend time intentionally getting outside our normal social patterns. How do you create that space/time? Following is a list of strategies to help break those patterns that become big old ruts in our lives.

STRATEGY ONE: WORK WITHIN YOUR NORMAL AFFINITIES

I (Bob) enjoy the fire service, so I am a volunteer firefighter. Any time I am not on the road, I take the opportunity to run fire calls. This is a great, non-threatening way to build relationships with people. This is historically a group of people who are not part of churches. So after I have built on the relationship, there always seems to be an opportunity where I am able to share my faith story. Of course, this doesn't happen on the first or the second or even on the third conversation. I must spend time at the local firehouse running fire calls, attending social events, and hanging around in order to build trust and credibility with the people in the fire service.

When I (Bob) was in Celeste, Texas, I joined the Lions Club. This was not necessarily to be a Lion. It was the opportunity to hang around with different people outside the church. When I was in Lee's Summit, Missouri, I joined the Rotary Club, not to be a Rotarian, but to hang out with different people in a different social circle. When I was in St. Peters, Missouri, I joined the Chamber of Commerce, not necessarily to be a member, but to hang out with a different social circle. I joined each of these organizations to enjoy people, meet new people, and have the opportunity to start conversations and build relationships with new people. Remember, being a missionary requires building trust in your community. I am reminded of the common saying, "when in Rome, be Roman," when in Athens, be Greek.

Most of us Christians like being around other Christians for the most part. But if we are to meet new, unconnected people who do not know Jesus Christ, we will need to hang out in places or in organizations where there are people who are unconnected to the church. It is okay to spend some time in organizations composed of Christians, but make it a priority to find places to hang out that are not chock full of Christians. It is necessary to evaluate how we are investing our time. What are the results of that investment of time? The church is not paying me (Bob) to ride a fire truck (or to play golf or to construct buildings for Habitat for Humanity), but if that time investment results in bringing people to Jesus Christ, it is well worth it. When you have attended a group for a year, ask yourself if you are seeing anyone become a part of the faith community as a result of your time investment in that group. If the answer is no, you need to evaluate your technique and/or whether it is the right group in which to invest your time.

If you are a golfer, you are going to hang out at the golf course. If you like coffee, you will hang out at the local coffee shop. Other places and ways to hang out could be scrapbooking stores/groups, travel clubs, PTA, booster club, softball, walking the dog, running, car clubs, motorcycle clubs, fishing, hunting, or camping.

We think God works best through you when you are doing things you enjoy. You are doing something you enjoy and are around others who enjoy that activity, too. God gave you that affinity to work through you! Be open to the opportunities your affinity provides for connection with others. The following is a list of other opportunities or events where you might be able to connect with people you do not already know.

STRATEGY TWO: MEMBER-GUEST EVENTS (CHURCH)

Member-guest events are events organized by the church. In order for a church member to participate in the event, the member must bring along an unconnected guest to participate in the event. For example, your church plans a golf event, and you must bring an unconnected guest with you or you cannot participate. This guest would be someone who does not attend the church. Look at your F.R.A.N. list for possible people to invite (Friends, Relatives, Acquaintances/Associates, and Neighbors).

Other possible member-guest events might include a fishing trip, a 5K run/walk, a bicycle or motorcycle outing, dinner for eight (four are members and four are guests), mother-daughter teas, basketball or volleyball tournaments, and softball teams. The options are endless. We may be able to take a current fellowship event with an inward focus and turn it into an outwardly focused member-guest event by always including a guest with each member. Look at all of your current social ministries and find a way to expand them to invite and include unconnected guests. Every ministry event should include a plan to include bringing unconnected guests, the welcoming of guests, and the inclusion of guests into our church ministry.

STRATEGY THREE: WORK OUTSIDE YOUR COMFORT ZONE

Jesus walked along the border of Samaria. He didn't always take the shortest route. He often took the least desirable route. He spent a great deal of his time outside the "safety zone." He purposely put himself in places to meet new people. He purposely put himself in circumstances that others ignored or even steered clear of engaging in. He didn't create a routine and get stuck. His course was ever changing to bring more and more people into the faith. Jesus was always widening the circle of influence and connectivity to people that the established church did not already know.

Put yourself in places you don't normally go. Spend some of your time in your un-comfortable zone. The more you do that, the easier it will be to do this in your affinity groups. Use this opportunity to practice. My wife and I (Bob) really go outside of our comfort zone when we hang out in motorcycle clubs. But it gives us the opportunity to hang out with people we don't know and people who are very different from us.

What might you do to break your routine? Could you place yourself where you are more likely to meet new, unconnected people? How might you place yourself outside your own comfort zone? Too often, we think about our faith only on Sundays. We need to deepen our lives by seeing the ordinary days as extraordinary possibilities to reach people with our faith. How can we create opportunities to share our faith with others as we go about our everyday life? "Faith" doesn't just happen at church; it happens everywhere, all the time.

STRATEGY FOUR: CREATE MARGINS IN YOUR LIFE

Our lives are full! People are busy! Their calendars are full! Their "to do lists" are unending. Their family activities are endless. We would most likely deem people lazy or crazy if they told us their day consisted of some prayer, some scripture reading, meditating, and then meeting some new, unconnected people at the coffee shop to share their faith stories. Our culture has conditioned us to think that this lifestyle is unfathomable if not impossible. We just have too much going on to be authentic Christians. So we tend to compartmentalize our church life, separating it from the rest of our everyday lives. We think missions rather than being missional.

What if something in between were possible? We are not suggesting that you do nothing else but share your faith. While that would be an admirable choice, most people would not find that to be a viable one. But are we willing to slow down our lives a bit to create opportunities? Are we willing, as disciples of Christ, to create spaces in our lives, to notice other people in our pathway? Culture is driving us away from some space or margin in our lives. Create margin in your life that is not rushed or packed with activity. It is actually countercultural to have that margin.

Let's look to Jesus as an example. Jesus created margins in his life. After he was raised from the dead, he stopped at the shoreline to visit with the fishermen/disciples. He built a fire, cooked fish, and invited the fishermen/disciples to join him. You would have thought he might have been a bit pressed to get on to Heaven, but he stopped and took time to build relationships. He stopped during the parade to talk to Zacchaeus. He began his ministry at a wedding social engagement at his mother's request. Jesus didn't have any trouble changing his busy schedule to engage with people in their social circles, which were not necessarily his social circles. How many times were Jesus' disciples pressing him to move on when Jesus lingered to talk to and minister to people outside his and the disciples' social circle? Jesus understood and practiced engaging with others through the intentional margins he created in his life. A disciple's life is a life of interruptions!

Just think how different life might be if it included margins. Not only would we be living out what Christ asked of us, but we would be more attuned to our surroundings and our loved ones. Sometimes it seems as if the church has filled our lives with busy-ness and we have missed the real heart of the faith, which is building authentic relationships with the people we love *and* the unconnected people we don't know yet.

For example when I (Bob) was in seminary, I pastored the Celeste charge of churches in Texas. One year, I decided to drive a bus for the local school district. I decided to do this because everybody told me there were no children in the community, and there were indeed very few children in the churches. Yet there was an elementary school in town that had three bus routes. So I figured if I drove one of the three school buses for a year, I would get to know where the children lived, who the children were, and what social circles the children and their families engaged in. After one year of driving the bus, a third of the students from my bus ended up coming to one of my churches. Had I not created the margin to drive the bus, I would have never engaged in those social circles and would have missed the opportunity to reach the children and their families.

STRATEGY FIVE: ROUTINE INTRODUCTIONS AND HANDING OUT BUSINESS CARDS

As pastor, go to every business in your mission field at least twice a year. (Lay people could do this as well.) Introduce yourself. Simply say, "If I can be helpful in any way, please give me a call." Leave your business card. They will most likely never call with a need. But people will begin to recognize you out in the community as that pastor who came by to introduce him or herself. In larger cities, you might have to pick a certain geographic area to concentrate your efforts. Be sure to create handouts or business cards for laity to use as well. The card can note them as a lay missioner from church.

Once or twice a year, deliver donuts or cookies to the businesses in your community. These should be delivered by lay people with warm smiles from your congregation. Drop the treats off and let the people there know you want to support the local businesses. Again ask, "Is there anything we can do to be helpful?" Put a note on the box of donuts with the same message and contact information. This will let others know who the donuts are from and why. Both the handing out of business cards to local businesses and drop offs are great ways for laity to practice sharing their faith by relational evangelism through service (elementary evangelism).

STRATEGY SIX: CREATE HANGOUT PLACES

Create your own hangout places. Make frequent visits to five different places in your community, to get to know unconnected people and build relationships with them. Talk with the manager. Get to know the manager. Get to know other patrons. Go the same time each day to build relationships with other customers. If you hit your hangout place about the same time each day, you will likely have the same employees helping/serving you each time. If you are buying from them, the door is open to get their names. Write their names down and follow up. What is the follow-up process? You could friend them on Facebook or link to them on other social media, send them a note, give them a call, or invite them back to the same location for more conversation. Pastors, do your sermon preparation at your hangout place. Laity, hold your Bible study or team meeting there as well. Create as many acquaintances as possible.

As an example, when I (Bob) was serving Church of the Shepherd, I moved the traditional pastor's Bible study to the Mid Rivers Mall in St. Peters, Missouri. Each week when we gathered in the coffee shop, more people joined the group. People came in to order coffee and then leaned in to listen to our conversation from across the table. Remember, people in America are spiritually hungry. They are just scared to go to church. They do not necessarily equate spirituality and the church. Get your church out of the building as much as possible!

Do business at the same gas station, grocery store, dry cleaner, and car wash. Patronize the same places all the time so that you can meet new, unconnected people, build relationships, and be open to opportunities to share.

STRATEGY SEVEN: SLOW DOWN AND OFFER BLESSINGS

Slow your life down enough to bless someone each day and maybe start a conversation. Don't just blow through places and aisles. Notice the other people around you. You may just be in that particular place at that particular time for a particular unconnected person whom God needs you to meet. People want to be noticed. People want to know they matter. Make a point to bless someone every day. Thank the cashier for a great job she did on processing your order. Acknowledge the sacker for being careful of how the bags were placed in the cart with care.

I (Bob) was at the Atlanta airport. My flight was delayed. I was bored and angry. I decided to go into one of the airport restaurants to kill some time. I asked to be placed at a table near the window so I could watch planes come and go. I was seated next to a table full of noisy kids. Their parents were sitting across the aisle in another booth. So here were four kids in the booth by themselves. Of course, my first thought was all about how I didn't want to sit by these noisy kids. I was already in a foul mood. I just wanted some peace and quiet. But as I began to watch this family, I grew amazed at the great parenting that I was witnessing. The parents were able to guide these children and their behavior without ever leaving their booth. It was a wonderful thing to watch. As the family got up to leave the restaurant, I took the opportunity to tell those parents what great parenting skills they demonstrated and what great twin boys they had. Of course, the mother beamed from ear to ear to be acknowledged for a job well done. And those boys were quite proud of themselves, too. Every opportunity is an opportunity to bless!

If you are putting gas in your car, take the opportunity to go inside the station or convenience store. Even if you pay at the pump, go inside anyway. Buy a soda. You want to encounter people at the counter. You become the local pastor when people repeatedly see you, and that happens when you take the time to converse with people. Local means being a bit loco (crazy!). Are you willing to be a little bit "loco" for Jesus?

STRATEGY EIGHT: ORGANIZATION CONNECTION STRATEGIES

Make sure you get to know your local civic leaders. Routinely visit the police station, fire station, mayor's office, community services, principals, superintendents, county office, city office, and sheriff. Introduce yourself and ask what you can do to be helpful. Always leave your card for them to contact you.

SUMMARY

Remember, our business is people and Jesus and Jesus and people. Building a bridge between the two is the business of the church. It is much easier for a guest to walk into church on the elbow of a friend than to walk in all alone as a stranger. If our guests for worship already know us, they will more likely look over some of our other challenges. If our music isn't top notch or the sermon is boring, it won't matter as much. People who already know someone in the church are more likely not to be such hard graders. They are there because of their already-established relationships.

Church is about people and Jesus. People are our main business. There is no one strategy that works best. It is at best a culmination of many things and many people working together. Some things will work better than others will. The point is to get out of the church and to look for opportunities to engage unconnected people in conversation. The best tactic is a multitude of relationship opportunities. We have to start being intentional about building a culture of expectation and experimentation as we try new things. Otherwise, we will stay in our church cocoon and wonder where everyone is.

So if everyone invited someone to church as often as you do, how would your church be doing? To take it a step further, if everyone started a conversation with the un-churched as often as you do, how would the church be doing? If the business of the church is Jesus and people, how is business? In the next chapter, we will explore how to move people from casual acquaintances to authentic "real" relationships, to give us an opportunity to have a conversation and create the possibility for them to participate in the community of faith.

MOVING FROM ACQUAINTANCE TO AUTHENTIC RELATIONSHIP

In a recent church facility conversation, church members and leaders were excited about their upcoming lobby renovation project. They were sure that once the new lobby was completed, new people would arrive at their church. The community would just rush into the church as a result of this renovation. How often we think that doing some sort of facility project will solve all our problems! We hang onto the common misconception that if only we were to tweak this one thing, all would be right with the world. Or that if we build something new, they will come.

The attraction model alone is dead. Building a new building, putting a new product inside the building, hanging a sign out front saying "You all come" was an effective strategy in the'80s and '90s if you wanted to reach more people for your congregation. But the attraction model rarely reached *new* people. Instead, it most often re-connected disconnected Christians who were bored or burned out in the mainline churches. You do need to have your church ready for guests. But preparing the church building for guests without extending a personal invitation will rarely result in guests showing up on their own. So it is imperative that we learn how to network in our mission fields so that we can build authentic relationships with unconnected people and lead them to connect with our faith communities.

Remember, you are building trust.

The missing element in our church strategies (if we have any strategy at all) is connecting with unconnected people. Expecting people to show up just because we renovated the lobby is like setting an extra plate at the table and expecting an extra guest to show up for dinner. If we want guests for dinner, we need to invite them. If the church really wants guests to show up for its ministries, we must spend a great deal of time in the mission field building relationships with unconnected people. We are not suggesting high-pressure or sales tactics, but rather to start real conversations with real people to build real relations that lead to a real experience with Jesus Christ in the gathered faith community. How do you talk to someone in a more normal, authentic, non-threatening way? None of us wants to look like an idiot! We don't want to be obnoxious. In the last chapter, we explored ways to create opportunities for those real conversations with real people. In this chapter, we will discover ways to have those conversations, to build authentic relationships with unconnected people.

If we were to meet someone for the first time in a convenience store and then invited that person to dinner, he or she would think we were absolutely crazy! Why would someone you'd just met invite you to his or her house for dinner? There is no relationship. There is no trust. It would feel strange and awkward, to say the least. Yet this is what we have sometimes been trained to do—to meet people and tell them they ought to come to our church. They won't come! How meaningful is an invitation from someone they don't know or trust?

We all need to quit trying to sell the church. We don't need to sell God. We are building relationships with new people, and those new people will enrich our experiences with God. As Martha Grace Reese says in *Unbinding the Gospel: Real Life Evangelism*, "Once you have a rich faith life and a healthy church, your questions shift from, 'Why would I do *evangelism*' to 'Oh, Lord, how can I help people see your face. Show me today, lead me to the ones you can reach through me. Let me be part of what you want to do next'" (Atlanta: Chalice Press, 2008, p. 66).

Reese says that "a huge number of mainline church members and pastors feel awkward, embarrassed, uncomfortable, defensive or angry when evangelism is mentioned" (p. 9). So how do we move past the discomfort into helping others see the face of Christ? The following is a simple process for moving from the initial conversations with new, unconnected people to a deeper, authentic relationship.

STEP ONE: LISTEN FOR THEIR STORY

Step One begins after the initial conversation described in Chapter Five. This step requires you to listen carefully to the person you've just met. Ask good, open-ended questions that allow the opportunity for the person to tell you more about his or her life. You want to demonstrate authentic interest in the other person. Make sure the questions are relevant to the other person, the circumstances, and your shared interest/common ground. Show a sincere attitude of curiosity about the other person. One question will lead to the next, like peeling back the layers of an onion. An answer to one question leads to the next question. Resist the urge to make it about you and your story. Give the other person the opportunity to share his or hers. Have fun with this. It is all about making a connection with another person. It is all about giving other people the opportunity to talk about themselves and learning about them and how you might connect to them. This is about building a relationship that might possibly go to the next level. It is just like a normal conversation that progresses as you learn more about one another. It is not a contrived conversation. It should feel and sound authentic to you and the other person. Go with the flow of the conversation!

Remember Bob's Harley story in Chapter Five? This conversation was natural. It flowed. It was not contrived or mechanical. The other person was highly engaged and didn't feel Bob was obnoxious or pushy. He was happy to talk about motorcycles and Mustangs. In fact, he wanted to go to a church that was led by a Harley-riding pastor!

STEP TWO: WATCH FOR SIGNALS

Step Two occurs when the other person becomes curious about you. It is the opportunity to share your faith in relevant ways. It opens the door to take the conversation to the next level. If you've done Step One well (listened closely and peeled back the onion layers with good questions), this step will occur naturally. If the conversation in Step One has been unique and refreshing, the person is very likely to ask a question and open this door.

The "end question" you might arrive at (hopefully) is asking if that person has a church home. If not, you then have the opportunity to invite him or her. Sometimes the conversation will naturally flow to arrive at the end question. Other times it may not. Sometimes you will never get to the end question because it is only a short, one-time encounter with someone. Other times this conversation will occur over a period of time—days, week, months, or even years.

> **This is more intuitive than mechanical.**

The "end question" may come through the curiosity of the other person asking what you do and why you do it. It's the Who, What, When, Where, Why, and How questions. When you are trying to shift to the end question, remember it is more intuitive than mechanical. When you begin to answer the end question, do not be afraid to say you are a pastor or identify yourself as a lay person from a particular church. A special note to the laity/lay missioner: don't forget to identify yourself as a lay leader from a particular congregation. Otherwise, people will not make the natural connection of what you are representing. For example, I (Kay) long ago in a conversation would have introduced myself as a member of Christ Church. Now I would introduce myself as a coach and lay missioner from Christ Church.

Be brave enough to tell the person your story. This is relational evangelism at the graduate level. Now, remember every conversation goes differently. There is no way to predict where a conversation turns, how a conversation ends, or what leads you to the next conversation. Again, this is more intuitive than mechanical—more art than science. Be brave enough to take the journey. What is the worst thing that can happen? Sometimes the conversation simply draws to a close without a conclusion, and you compliment the other person or acknowledge or bless him or her in some way. Be at peace! Hopefully, not all of your conversations simply come to a close. If they do, re-evaluate your approach. Some of your conversations should, in fact, result in invitations and engagement in your faith community, but that rarely happens in the first conversation. Remember, we are building a relationship, not an encounter.

STEP THREE: BRIDGE-BUILDING PHRASES

It is important to learn how to use your conversation to build bridges that might lead people to the faith community. You can do this in a way that feels comfortable and natural, without being obnoxious. There are words and phrases that can bridge your conversations, allowing you to share the who and why. The who for Bob is, "I am a United Methodist pastor." The who for Kay is, "I am a church coach and lay missioner from Christ Church." The who for Doug is, "I work with churches to help them share God's love."

While this is relatively easy for pastors because of their position with the church, it is not always comfortable for the lay person, who may be unsure how to characterize his or her role. A good phrase to use to introduce yourself is, "I am a lay missioner from (my church)." When we name our role in the church, it allows us to transition into the why of the story. For instance, we might say, "I spend a good amount of my time getting to know new people." The bridge statement won't necessarily be the same each time. It has to flow with the conversation. You have to be comfortable with your own words. This process is not science. It is an art. Sometimes this art is natural, and other times it must be learned. It may be easier for extroverts than introverts. But it can be learned. Practice in safe places like your small groups, Bible studies, and Sunday school classes (sharing you faith in a group—middle school evangelism). The more you practice in safe places with friends, the more comfortable you will be in spontaneous conversations with unconnected people in your community. Experiment with different questions and bridge statements. You will find your own rhythm and words when you just get out there and begin doing it.

Remember, Step One (listening for their story) is always Step One. But the other steps are not necessarily in sequence. The sequence may be different with different conversations. Learn to dance in the conversation, to know which step flows with the conversation based on where people are in their faith journeys, their comfort level with you, and the circumstances of the conversation.

STEP FOUR: KNOW YOUR ELEVATOR STORY

Step Four is exploring how God's story is a vital part of our stories. This is about knowing your faith story. It is about knowing where you have seen God at work in your life. It is having your two-minute "elevator speech" ready. As a business person, I (Kay) have to have a very clear, concise way to explain what

I do when someone asks. You have less than two minutes to communicate who you are and what you do. In the business world, we refer to this as an elevator speech because you should be able to give your speech to someone riding with you from one floor to the next. But have you ever considered your faith elevator speech? How would you tell someone in a clear, concise way about your faith story?

As Adam Hamilton says in *Leading Beyond the Walls*, we must also be able to answer three big questions: Why God? Why the church? Why my church? (Nashville: Abingdon, 2002). The following is Bob's version of how he might answer these three questions for an unconnected seeker.

WHY GOD?

I (Bob) grew up in the church and have believed in God my whole life. My faith life has not been a constant forward-moving journey. There have been both mountain and valley experiences and even some desert experiences. When I look back over my lifetime, I see the hand of God in my life, and I realize it wasn't all my doings. Remember, I am an American, therefore I have been trained to think-individualism I did it all by myself. Remember in America, individualism is a strong cultural value. Left to my own devise, I would think that everything that happened to me was because of my own hand – a self made man. But when I put that against the reflection of God, I realize that is not true. These "other hand" moments have occurred through numerous events, people, and experiences in my life. What would be another answer to why these events have happened in my life? To me, there is no other answer. It has to be God! For me, it is always easier to see God in the rearview mirror instead of the windshield.

Now keep in mind the number one road block to people believing in God is that if there is a good God, how could a good God allow all this bad stuff to happen in the world? This is the burning question of the unconnected. I believe God wants wonderful things to happen in our lives. God is in charge but not in control. If God were fully in control, we would be robots. God gave us free will. We are not robots. We get to run our lives and make our own choices. People have heard over and over again that God is in control and brings all these bad things into your life to teach lessons. For me that is not true. God wants good things for me, not bad. Now this is not to say that my life lessons have not come from disappointment. They do. But if God is a good God, then good is what God wants. Not bad. Most bad comes from my own choices when I am not paying attention to the life lessons taught in Scriptures. The church helps us create healthy boundaries to keep us on track with our free will. My church gives me the relationships and support to keep my free will on track. Faith is relevant. It gives you the axis for life.

That is the end of my two-minute elevator speech unless I'm asked to share more, and then I go into my answer on "why church."

WHY CHURCH?

You may believe in God, but why bother with the church? If you look at the church in its centuries of existence, how could all these millions of people believe in God if it weren't true? Smarter people than me have studied, written, and experienced God for centuries through the church. I have traveled on missionary trips to India, South Africa, Russia, Korea, China, Mozambique, Alaska, and Mexico—all very different people. All very different cultures. All very different languages. Separated by thousands of miles. Yet they have all experienced God. They have set up some sort of church in the communities that were changing lives and transforming their part of the world. Even though they all worship differently, they all still believe in God. When you look at the church at its best, it is the most hopeful thing that happens in the world. Through the church, I too had my life transformed by God. Through the church, I found purpose, meaning, and vital relationships for my life. The church is one of the instruments that God has used to confirm God's existence on planet Earth.

I would be the first to admit that the church is filled with a flawed group of people (including myself). When you look over the church's history, during the times in which the church gets absolute power (church-state empires), bad things tend to happen. Remember, the church is the one that crucified Christ. The church beheaded people for their beliefs. The church initiated the Crusades. The church burned witches at the stake in America. The church defended slavery. The church has abused children and adults and had many moral failures. When we become the center of power, the church tends to do bad things and makes horrendous decisions. Power and church don't go well together. Humility and church together work best. There is much criticism of the church today based on these and other historical events that really happened and reflect badly on the church. And they are true. When the mainline church in America became the center of American culture, "church-centric," we became an institution instead of a missional move-ment of Jesus Christ. It is leading us to our own demise. Jesus is the way, the truth, and the life. Jesus is not religion. Jesus is the way. Jesus is not an institution. John Wesley said Methodism is a way of living. When the church gets power and influ-ence, it tends to self-corrupt, and I think it leads us away from what God intends the church to be. The church is one of God's instruments for the transformation of the world. When compared to other organizations and most governments, the church's overall track record is quite good, though it is flawed.

Because the church is God's instrument, I just won't give up. I believe the church is the hope of the world and Jesus is the salvation of the world. I still believe the church is the training ground for human beings to live beyond themselves and find their own purpose and meaning while on planet Earth. When the church decides to come together, it can make an incredible difference in people's lives and in the world. I have seen it and I have experienced it. For instance, the United Methodist Church and the Bill Gates Foundation came together over five years with a goal of reducing malaria in Africa. Together, we initiated a program called "Nothing But Nets." For $10, you could purchase a mosquito net that would be given to an individual in Africa to hang over a bed. The Bill Gates Foundation quickly figured out the very best delivery mechanism in Africa was the local church, rather than clinics, governments, and non-profits. In this case, it happened to be the Methodist Church. It was the local church that was on the ground with the people. Because of this connection, the infection rate of malaria in Africa has been reduced by one third. When the church decides to do God's work, great things can happen!

Now, if the conversation deepens and people ask why your church, you should be ready with your church story. The following is Bob's answer to this question.

WHY MY CHURCH?

I think the community of faith provides focus for our individual lives and possible transformation for communities in the world. I believe there is no such thing as an isolated Christian. Jesus always led people back to a gathered faith community. Our faith is most vitally lived out in connection with others. What makes the gospel the gospel is the cross of Jesus Christ. The cross reminds us that it is a relationship between God and me, but it is more than just God and me. I do need the vertical relationship with God. But I also need the horizontal relationship, in which I reach out to others with Christ. That makes the cross. When people are involved in a gathered faith community (church), it makes such a difference in individual lives. It is where people find meaning, purpose, rhythm, support, and accountability to live their lives to the fullest. I just can't imagine going through life by myself without this community of believers.

I think people need connection. Even though we are so technology-driven, digitally driven, individually driven, there is still a genuine craving for human *beings to experience something together that is bigger than ourselves and in a common direction. Why else would 76,000 people gather at a football stadium, soccer stadium, or basketball court? Why else would people purchase Diet Coke for $8 or a hot dog for $10 in a stadium, when they could have one at home for a fraction of the cost? The reason is because human beings crave momentum in their lives. They need a gathered experience. They need to feel the win. When we go to a sports stadium, we are all hoping for the same things. Going the same direction. Cheering for the same result. When we get a win, we are exhilarated. When we have a loss, we are depressed. After a sports team wins or loses, you can see and feel it in the attitudes of an entire metropolitan area. Why is this? Because God has designed us to experience energy when we participate in community.*

People crave connection and momentum.

Isn't it interesting that God displayed Godself as Father, Son, and Holy Spirit? One in three and three in one. It even sounds like a cheer. God lives in community. One of the reasons I continue to encourage us to lead others back to the gathered faith community is because God is best and most easily experienced in the faith community. The gathered worship experience is the best place to experience God. When a church gets it right, worship provides that spark and motivation to get through the week. We can get out of that rhythm of church very easily. The church should inspire people. If they walk away from the church wanting, we have missed a very fundamental, deep thing. Much like the NFL/ MLB, we must inspire.

Mainline Christians tend to fear that they'll be asked to go out on their own into the mission field and convert someone. That is not relational evangelism. Relational evangelism points people back to the faith community, allowing God's Holy Spirit to work through the worship experience to touch and change people's lives. Let the Holy Spirit do the heavy lifting. Not us. We are the bridge to the gathered community. The church is the hope of the world, not the salvation. Jesus is the salvation. Start a conversation today!

KAY'S REFLECTION

As a lay person, it was very interesting for me to hear Bob's answers to the three "big questions." We have spent many hours talking about church "stuff" over the past three years as we have worked together on our books and in the HCI process, but I had never heard his answers to these questions before. What I find most interesting is his questioning of the existence of God. I guess I had never considered the idea that a pastor would have these same thoughts as I have experienced in the ups and downs in my life. Hearing his answer to "Why God?" it seems to me that this might help break down the perceived depth of the "Why God?" question for laity. I think people of faith are scared to share their faith because they are concerned about people asking them about their Bible knowledge. But people are really just asking why you choose to believe in God, why you think there is a need/desire for church, and why should they be interested in participating in your local church. These are not huge theological questions. These are the heart-felt, soul-filled answers that describe your personal stories of why you choose to walk the Christian pathway and continue to choose the church.

STEP FIVE: KNOWING YOUR FAITH STORY

Step Five is not talking about your church history. This is not your membership status. This step is about recalling your personal faith story. It is about your personal experience with Jesus Christ. Most of us have lost our story or have never discovered it.

When we conduct church consultations, one of the interview questions for pastors and leaders is about their spiritual journey. Rarely do they tell us about their spiritual journey. They talk instead about their church history/affiliation. We seem to compartmentalize our lives. We have our church lives and then our lives out in the secular world. We don't see these as being all woven together. Our goal is to be authentic Christians, weaving relational evangelism as a lifestyle. Our lifestyle should encompass being a missionary. Yet we often seem to talk about our faith only in church settings.

When we talk about a personal spiritual journey, we are referring to how and where God has worked or is working in your life. Where are you seeing God at work in your own life or those of the people around you? What are those pivotal times in your life when you had a personal encounter with God? What was happening? What were you thinking? How did that encounter affect you? When we begin to rediscover these moments in our lives and be more attentive to looking for them today and tomorrow, we will be able to share this with others. For when we are able to answer the question "Where have you seen God lately?" we are able to be the face, hands, ears, and eyes for God as we were intended to be.

STEP SIX: FIND THE NEED AND CONNECT NEW PEOPLE WITH NEW PEOPLE

Step Six is connecting your acquaintances to other people in the church in order to build authentic relationships with other new people in the congregation. Through building those relationships, we will discover their needs and connect them to ministries in our congregation to satisfy their needs. Remember, the most important thing the church has to offer is relationships—relationships with each other and with Christ. That connection could be made with an invitation to worship, small group, a church event, a hands-on mission experience, and so on. This should be a situation in which people can step in easily, without a lot of obstacles. Be sure to ask, "Would you like to come *with* me?" This isn't about sending people off on their own. We have to make the connection for them. This is an experience you will walk through with them and have the opportunity to connect them with other people of faith. Walk the road with them. Not only will this provide more of a chance of the person indeed connecting, but it will also give you a story to share with the next new person you encounter. It will also deepen your walk with Christ.

Isolation and loneliness are the biggest problems people face today. So how can we provide relationships to overcome those feelings of isolation and loneliness? How can we meet people's needs? What are the on-ramps at your church for new people? What are the places and events where your church can offer opportunities for new people to connect? Guests need a long on-ramp for them to connect into the life of the church. They can't go from zero to 65 in one small step. So we have to provide multiple opportunities for unconnected guests and new believers to connect in our churches. Keep asking them how we can be more helpful. To move someone from acquaintance to friend will most likely require multiple conversations over time. Remember, we are building real, authentic relationships. This won't all happen at once. Be patient. Be consistent. Be persistent. Don't be afraid to make some mistakes. It is better to try and make some mistakes than not to try at all.

SUMMARY

Remember this process helps people move from being unconnected acquaintances to people who are connected into the life of the congregation. Step One is Step One, but the others may not happen in any particular order. Most likely, conversations will mature over time. It may be two conversations, ten conversations, or a hundred conversations. This is about building authentic relationships. You may at times not get to finish the conversation. You may be a seed planter for the kingdom of God. It is more about the kingdom and less about your church.

Are you willing to create spaces in your life, to have conversations with unconnected people whom you don't know? Conversations that might lead them to an authentic relationship with you, that might lead them across the faith line, that might lead them to the gathered faith community? You have to have a willingness to spend time with people you don't know for results you might not see. One thing is for certain—if you don't do any of this, you will certainly have no results!

In the first section, we presented some ways to share your faith in safe places. In this second section, we hope you gained new ideas and practices to start conversations with unconnected people, leading to authentic relationships and faith conversations that result in people coming to a community of faith. In the next section, we will help the church be prepared for guests, to create a culture of hospitality that leads people on a faith journey.

CREATE AN OUTWARDLY FOCUSED CULTURE

Are you ready for guests in your congregation? In Section One, we learned how to find our story and how to share our story in safe places, and we got ready to share our story with unconnected people. In Section Two, we learned how to put ourselves in places where we could meet new people, unconnected people. We learned how to start conversations with unconnected people. We learned how to build authentic relationships with unconnected people. We learned to share our faith with unconnected people and to invite them to participate in the faith community. But all of that work does no good if the congregation is not ready for guests when they arrive. Remember, the number one road block for connected people inviting unconnected people to worship is that they are not confident in the experience guests will have when they do arrive. To get ready, we must have a willingness to change.

Are we willing to change our likes and preferences to reach our grandchildren? We find time after time that people in our dying congregations like the way things are. That is, they like the building, the worship service, the music, the fellowship, the ministries. At the same time, they are quick to add, "We just need some young people to come." They truly want to have young people in their churches. Everybody wants young people in their churches, but most are unwilling to make the changes necessary to reach those young people. We are happy to have young people come as long as it doesn't change anything other than the number of folks sitting in the pews for worship. So let us ask, "How's that working for you?"

To reach the unconnected new people, we must develop a new culture. This new culture will be one of adapting and change. The church will need to adapt its culture to be more hospitable to guests. For the most part, churches are friendly. We truly enjoy our relationships with our friends in the congregation. We are friendly with one another. This is fellowship. Most churches have great fellowship. We enjoy engaging and investing time with those we already know authentically. Many times, however, guests feel differently when they come into a congregation for the first time. A guest would not necessarily feel the friendliness. If guests walked into your church on Sunday morning, would they feel as though they just walked into your family's Thanksgiving dinner? Would they feel awkward and out of place? Would they feel like they were intruding? Would they know the insider stories and language? Would they feel as though they were a fifth wheel at this gathering?

We must transition ourselves from being solely focused on friendliness and fellowship to centering on hospitality, RADICAL hospitality. Hospitality is something we offer or extend to make others feel welcome, part of the group, and comfortable: a greeting, a cup of coffee, and directions to the sanctuary. These are all things that one might expect as a guest, whether it be at your home or at church. But radical hospitality takes it to another dimension. Radical hospitality is going above and beyond. Radical hospitality is exceeding expectations. To learn more about radical hospitality, see *The Five Practices of Fruitful Congregations* by Bishop Robert Schnase.

Radical hospitality is exceeding expectations.

To provide radical hospitality, churches will most likely need to create an intentional process to make sure it is accomplished each and every time the door opens. We need a culture of radical hospitality that is ingrained and practiced everywhere all the time and not just for the worship experience. It will take training and time for radical hospitality to be fully developed. People in the congregation will be challenged to move past fellowship with those they already know so that they are available to serve in hospitality roles, allowing the church to extend radical hospitality to all guests.

One thing we have all had to learn is that the worship experience is not just about us (those of us who are already Christian or connected). We have learned from watching places such as Saddleback Church in Anaheim, California, that church is the main instrument God uses to reach people who are not already followers of Christ, or the unconnected. We Christians who attend worship are not just there to feed ourselves. Rather we, the connected, are missionaries to those arriving who do not yet know Jesus Christ—the unconnected. This is a hard shift for mainline Christians because we were taught that Sunday morning *was* indeed about us. So much so that we absorb most of our good leaders into adult Sunday school classes rather than making them available to assist those arriving who do not know Jesus Christ. We might even have to consider having our Sunday school meet at a time other than Sunday so that we can make ourselves available to serve in ministry on Sunday for guests. These ministries include not only radical hospitality but also music ministry and children's ministry. These are the three "Wow's" every congregation needs to have during the worship experience. Again, this is a hard shift for us mainliners. If Methodists were to rediscover our roots in John and Charles Wesley and Francis Asbury, we would find that adult learning occurred during the week in classes, bands, and what we might call small groups today. It is imperative for us to rediscover our roots so that we might receive new people in the twenty-first century.

The greatest gift the church has to give away is relationships. These include relationships with God, our relationships with each other, and our availability for relationships with people we do not know. People have an average of eight close relationships in the church. We tend to gravitate toward those people when we are in church or attending a church function. We could think of those eight relationships as the eight knobs on a Lego building block. Once those eight are full, we tend to spend time mostly with those eight people. What if this culture change challenged you to open up some of the knobs on your building block for new unconnected people—people who are looking for a faith community where they can find not just friendly people, but friends? Would you be willing to do this if it meant you might just be the pathway through which a guest finds a relationship with Christ?

Relationship Trinity: God, Others, Availability

It is not enough simply to make connections in worship. The fact is, we want people to have a deeper relationship with God. Once guests become regular attenders, we must provide an intentional discipleship pathway for them to grow closer in their relationship with Christ. How do people go about growing their faith in your church? Is there a pathway to help them along this journey? New people do best with other new people. So we need to make sure to have new connection points on a regular basis that allow new people to connect with other new people in their faith journey.

This next section explores ways to create a culture of hospitality, a process to make it happen, and an intentional discipleship pathway aimed at moving people deeper into a relationship with Christ.

LEADERSHIP MATTERS

Before a congregation can be open to a new perspective or culture, that openness must first be modeled by the church's leaders. To make a cultural shift, we must gather a group of passionate, enthusiastic people who want their church to be more missional and outwardly focused. Without this group of leaders and the pastor, it will be difficult to shift the perspective, culture, attitude, and ultimately the behavior of the congregation.

MISSION

The shift begins with a new understanding of the mission of the church. For the United Methodist Church, the Book of Discipline in Paragraph 122 describes the mission of the church as making new disciples of Jesus Christ for the transformation of the world. Jesus taught the disciples the mission.

> Then Jesus came to them and said, "All authority in heaven and on earth has been given to me. Therefore go and make disciples of all nations, baptizing them in the name of the Father and of the Son and of the Holy Spirit, and teaching them to obey everything I have commanded you. And surely I am with you always, to the very end of the age." (Matthew 28:18-20 NIV)

So how is the ministry of your church ordered to accomplish that one true purpose? We must be convicted that bringing unconnected people into a relationship with Jesus Christ is our true purpose, our mission. We must shift from an inwardly focused culture to an outwardly focused culture. The church must move from being about meeting the needs of those already attending (the connected) to an emphasis on those not yet attending (the unconnected). This outward focus stems from our sincere concern for the hearts and souls of those who do not yet have a relationship with Christ. We must not be happy and content solely with our existing friendships. We must also create availability in our lives, deep compassion for the unconnected— those who do not yet know Christ. We must have the desire to connect others to a gathered community of faith so that they, too, experience the love of God and each other. This is our purpose, our mission as the church. To accomplish it, our leaders must be willing to change.

VISION

We must also figure out how our individual churches live out the mission in their unique way. This living out of the mission is what we call the vision of a church. The vision of a church is the intersection of the passions of the leaders, the strengths of the congregation, and the needs of the community, according to Thom S. Rainer in his book *Breakout Churches: Discover How to Make the Leap* (Grand Rapids: Zondervan, 2005, p. 114). A good vision tells us how an individual church is going to live out the mission of the church. We must intentionally cast our vision for the unique way in which God is calling our church to live out the mission of making new disciples (see *Visioneering: God's Blueprint for Developing and Maintaining Vision* by Andy Stanley for more on creating a vision [Colorado Springs: Multnomah Books, 1999]). We recommend your local church leadership spend a third of its meetings on visioning. Leaders must also hold the church—and themselves—accountable for accomplishing the mission of the church by living into your church's vision. We have never seen a church grow because of a good mission and vision statement hanging on the wall. On the other hand, we have never seen a church grow that wasn't focused on its mission and vision.

GOALS

After we have accepted the mission and cast the vision, the church must focus itself toward living out the vision to accomplish the mission. What are the three or four goals for our church this year that will lead us into living out our vision and thus succeeding at our mission? We must determine the objectives to accomplish our annual goals. The objectives are the activities/ ministries of our congregation that will help us accomplish our goals. By accomplishing our goals, we will be living out the vision and accomplishing the mission. So we must structure ourselves to be missional. We do this primarily through strategic planning.

Strategic ministry planning must become part of the DNA of the church. The strategic ministry planning process includes five elements: mission, vision, core values, goals, and objectives. A great resource is *Strategic Ministry Planning*, a workbook by Kay Kotan, Ken Willard, and David Hyatt (found at www.Leadership4Transformation.com). Strategic planning conversations are centered on how decisions meet the mission, vision, and goals of the church while honoring the core values. Decision making becomes easier as it becomes aligned with a purpose, rather than based on tradition, church politics, or the calendar. The strategic plan is used every day to stay on track. Annually, the pastor and leaders must participate in a strategic planning process to evaluate the current year plan and create new goals and strategies for the upcoming year. Every three to five years, the vision should be re-evaluated and most likely recast.

EQUIPPING

It doesn't do any good to have a foundation if we don't have a plan to raise up new leaders from this foundation. What is your system for raising up leaders? Your church is only going to grow as fast as you raise up good leaders. It is vitally important for the pastor to move into a role of equipping people for ministry. Of course, this starts with equipping leaders to equip others. First, the pastor becomes the role model for becoming an outwardly thinking, outwardly focused congregation. Then, the pastor gathers a small group of current leaders (and most likely the next generation of leaders). The pastor will spend time getting to know this group, what gifts they have, what passions they possess, what life and vocational experience they bring, where they are in their spiritual journey, and how they interact with others. You might have them take a personality test such as DiSC, Myers-Briggs, or StrengthsFinder. The group should study church culture change and other relevant topics. Obviously, this will allow the pastor to get to know people. But more importantly, this will be a place where seeds can be planted to start the shift of cultural change.

> Your church is only going to grow as fast as you raise up good leaders.

MODELING

Once we have created a missional attitude with our leaders, the leaders can start modeling this with the congregation. New behaviors will be created that lead to the beginning of a shift to an outward focus of the congregation. Slowly, these leaders will begin to influence others in the congregation about the need of focusing on our mission field. As more and more in our congregation begin to understand our missional focus, a shift will begin in the culture of our congregation.

PREACHING

To create a culture of hospitality, teach and preach to it over and over (and over and over and over) again. Preach it until you are almost sick of it! We (Bob and Kay) live in Missouri in the land of the "Five Practices" (by Bishop Schnase), and we have shared and heard these practices seemingly ten million times. But as we work with individual congregations in Missouri, we find they are just now beginning to practice it—somewhat. Got to preach it 'til you see it!

> Got to preach it 'til you see it!

Building this foundation is a slow process. While you're building the foundation, you also need to practice some other congregation-wide strategies to help the congregation move to a missional attitude. Following are ten strategies that you could begin to practice. These strategies will help create early momentum as you are building this foundation. There are unlimited other possible strategies. Each congregation will need to discern which strategy will be most effective in their culture. Remember, the most effective way to connect new people to Jesus Christ is by becoming friends with people you do not know and then inviting them to the faith community. Personal invitation remains the number one way people connect to Christ.

FRIENDSHIP SUNDAYS

A couple of times a year, have a "Friendship Sunday" theme. Every regular attender should be encouraged to bring an unconnected friend. The sermon could have a friendship theme. You could include a special fellowship time before or after worship. Special gifts could be given to "friends." You could even hold a "friendly" contest to see who brings the most friends to worship.

F.R.A.N. PLAN

The F.R.A.N. Plan refers to Friends, Relatives, Acquaintances/Associates, and Neighbors and was developed by the Church Growth Institute. This process is intended to raise awareness of those unconnected people who are closest to us whom we sometimes forget to invite to worship. This program generally spans four different Sundays. Each Sunday, members of the church are challenged to bring unconnected guests to worship from one of the four categories listed. This process can be quite fun. You are limited only by your creativity.

Give people plenty of time to prepare for this challenge. Ask them to consider how many people they might be able to list in each category. Ask them to identify the people and to think about how they might extend the invitation. Ask the congregation and prayer team to pray over these unconnected guests coming for the next four weeks. Make sure the congregation is prepared to receive unconnected guests and extend radical hospitality.

While the first three categories are fairly straightforward, the category of neighbors might be quite narrow. Redefine the definition of neighborhood. Extend the thought of neighbors from being only those who live directly beside you to a more global vision of a neighborhood. It might also include places where you walk, places you shop, where the kids play kickball in the neighborhood, the neighborhood gym, Facebook, Starbucks, Panera, people you run with, the neighborhood convenience store, and the gas station.

We need constantly to evaluate how we develop those "acquaintance" relationships to a place where we can have the opportunity to talk about our faith. We might want to create opportunities to bring unconnected people as guests into our faith community that are less intimidating than a first step into worship. What are some easier steps to build relationships with these groups of unconnected people that offer something other than worship? Think about combining the challenge of your congregation inviting people using the F.R.A.N. process with a bridge event. (See the section on bridge events in Chapter Ten.)

MAJOR SUNDAYS

In Kennon Callahan's book *Twelve Keys to an Effective Church*, we are challenged to reconsider major Sundays. We tend to pull out all the stops for both our Easter and Christmas Eve services. And people do show up. We put our best foot forward and offer great music, teaching, preaching, and hospitality. We roll out the proverbial red carpet. So how might we do something even more extraordinary on those two Sundays?

What if we were to add two more major Sundays? For example, consider the Fourth of July. What could you do to create a Fourth of July that would be unforgettable? What could you do for Valentine's Day or Mother's Day or Father's Day or Veterans' Day or Back to School or Christmas in July? What would it look like to have a major Sunday each month? Pick out the next two Sundays with the highest attendance and consider how you could take it up a notch. Look at two or three years' worth of vital statistics trends to determine the attendance patterns. Spend your marketing, music, sermon series, and money on these highest-attendance days. The higher you can raise your high-attendance Sunday in a calendar year, the higher your low-attendance Sundays will also be. It is counterintuitive to strategize in this way. We tend to focus our energies on the four lowest-attendance Sundays of the year. You could do this, but it would require a great deal more energy and resources to have positive results. It is simply easier to raise your four highest attendances higher instead.

Make sure you follow a major Sunday with relevant Sundays. Consider "hot potato" topics for the sermons, and preach in a series. Create a reason for your guests to return. Create a sense of urgency for them to want to visit again. Present a topic that will fill a need in their lives if they return next week. Adam Hamilton refers to this type of sermon series as his "Fishing Expedition" in his book *Unleashing the Word*.

5-10-10 RULE

This "rule" challenges us to move out of our comfort zones and routines. For every five minutes you spend with someone you already know at church, spend ten minutes with someone you don't. Personally greet anyone within ten feet of you. Another way to work this process might be related to the number of people you have a relationship with. For every five people you know and talk to, spend time talking to ten people you don't know.

This process gives us goals and reminders to push us outside our comfort zone and see every opportunity to start a conversation with someone we don't know. Your church might create and hand out the rules on a card as a reminder. Not only will this be a reminder of the rules, but it will also remind us that we are missionaries. Sunday morning is about hospitality, not simply fellowship!

CHURCH-WIDE SUNDAY HOSPITALITY TRAINING

Rev. Jim Ozier from the North Texas Conference of the UMC teaches about the need to create church-wide hospitality training. He suggests one of the ways you create a new culture of hospitality is to train the entire congregation in hospitality at least twice a year. Keep the congregation mindful of the fact that hospitality is not extended by our greeters, ushers, and hospitality team only. A hospitality culture is not a "job" responsibility of only a few. Rather, radical hospitality becomes part of the DNA of a church. It is adopted as a value of the congregation. Rev. Jim Ozier is available to help your congregation with developing a culture of hospitality; contact him at ozier@ntcumc.org.

Remember, most guests arrive early or late. If they arrive late, the door is closed and everyone is engaged in worship. This includes the greeters! What happens to the guests? They are left to fend for themselves. Everyone is responsible for hospitality! We can't run hospitality training for a team once and think we have it covered. To create this culture, we must talk about it constantly and consistently. We must also train and equip our entire congregation on a regular basis. The training must provide the appropriate method to get a guest's name. We want the names for our record keeping, but we also want to create a culture in which the one greeting the guest might also personally follow up. This creates personal touches and opportunities for relationships and connections. Think of Southwest Airlines. It has created a culture of hospitality. The responsibility for hospitality does not lie only in the hands of the flight attendants. Hospitality extends from reservations, to the ticket counter, to baggage handlers, to pilots, to mechanics. It is the culture of the company. It is just the way they have decided to do business. It has become their niche in the airline industry.

> **Everyone is responsible for hospitality!**

If you don't have a hospitality team, start one today! That's the first step. This team can help begin to model the culture of hospitality throughout the congregation.

SKITS/DRAMA

During worship, conduct a skit or drama about how NOT to do hospitality. Make it funny! People learn through humor. The skit could include someone wandering around not able to find something. It could also include one person being ignored by everyone else, as "church insiders" are involved in conversations with each other. Include something about the insider language we use that could be misinterpreted or confusing to a guest. Another scenario could show the guest sitting in someone else's seat for worship.

MOVE FELLOWSHIP TO THE FRONT DOOR

How do you create a lobby experience at the front door? We need a place where people will want to "hang out." It could offer Wi-Fi, soft conversational seating, high-top tables, and something other than "church" coffee and donuts. Think of the Starbucks experience. The Starbucks mission statement is "to inspire and nurture the human spirit—one person, one cup and one neighborhood at a time." That mission, much like the mission of the church, is about nurturing the human spirit. How does your church begin to create this nurturing culture at the front door?

Many times, we serve coffee in our fellowship halls, which are traditionally in the basement. As regular attenders, we know where to find the coffee. But it might be a stretch for guests to figure this out. Another thing to consider is the possibility that if most of the congregation is in the basement having coffee after Sunday school or before worship, who is greeting our guests at the entrances? Moving fellowship to the front door not only allows guests to find the coffee, but it also provides the opportunity for guests to meet and connect with people in the congregation. Even if a greeter is at the door, there is not an inviting atmosphere when no one else is around.

What does it look like to move our fellowship to the front door? Does your current entrance feel like 1950, or does it create a new atmosphere for a new generation of people? Does it say "old church"? If the regulars are looking for their own friends and not paying attention to new people, it makes a new person feel left out or maybe even ignored. If we have the fellowship at the front door, it looks and feels like it is okay for everyone to hang out there. The problem is that most churches are not built to handle this at the front door. So you may have to remodel to make people feel comfortable hanging out here. Again, think Starbucks or Panera! The building footprint affects hospitality. We understand that the front entrances to most churches were created in a different era and for a different culture. It may take some time to reconfigure a more appropriate entrance for creating a culture of hospitality. This is worthy of a capital fundraising effort. In the meantime, you may need to resort to some creative ideas to overcome the shortcomings of your lobby, perhaps a pop-up tent outside as weather permits. This would alert people from the streets and create a new hospitality space just as an expansion of the lobby would. Everybody likes to be greeted. Every time you make people trek down the hall, you make them feel unwelcome, giving them a sense of not belonging. It's a mistake to assume that we are off the hook simply by placing greeters at our doorways.

HOSPITALITY DESK OR KIOSK (WELCOME CENTER)

Create a hospitality desk or kiosk inside the main entrance. Make sure someone is working the desk before, during, and after all church events. The desk should be supplied with extra bulletins and information on all the church ministries. The staff working the hospitality desk should be easily identifiable, with something like an "ask me" vest or name tag. The staff should also be well informed and knowledgeable about the building and all ministries. You could even consider installing a neon sign above the hospitality desk that says, "Start Here." Make sure the hospitality desk does not become covered up by flowers, food, or coffee. It should be easily identified and accessed by guests.

GO DIGITAL

Instead of bulletin boards hanging throughout the hallways of your church, consider going digital. Replace the bulletin boards with flat screen televisions near all entrances. Information can then be scrolled on these screens. No more messy tape, unprofessional flyers, or out-of-date information. Make sure the hallways are clutter-free with a nice coat of fresh paint on the walls. Please choose a color other than white! It is incredible what a gallon of paint can do to create momentum in your church.

THREE TOUCHES

From the time guests enter the parking lot until they sit down in the sanctuary, we want to provide a minimum of three touch points. What are three different interactions that a guest could have in your church? These could include the church entrance, the hospitality area, and the sanctuary. Other possibilities might include the parking lot, a person charged with the responsibility of connecting with guests, introduction to the pastor, introduction of other key staff, a children or youth ministry representative escorting the guest's children to the children's area, or someone presenting a gift to the guest. These personal touches are extremely important. We are striving for the guest to feel welcome but not overwhelmed. These touches should be sincere with good eye contact. The three touches are just the minimum. Keep asking yourself what happens next for the guest who visits your church.

At Saddleback Church, you are likely to find someone in the parking lot waving at you as you enter. At Church of the Resurrection, not only will you find someone in the parking lot guiding you to a parking spot but you will also find a greeter at every door (inside and out) as well as at every level of steps. Each greeter will extend a warm welcome, handshake, smile, assistance, bulletin, and help with finding a seat.

What happens at your church when a guest gets out of the car? What is the experience? Remember, three touches are the bare minimum.

SUMMARY

Of course, you can't implement all these suggestions at once. Choose a couple and try them out. If they work, that's great. Do them with excellence. If they don't work, try something else. Once you have one element up and working well, weave in another strategy. This doesn't happen overnight. But, with diligence and persistence, you can build a culture of hospitality starting with leadership.

YOUR BUILDING MATTERS

We find that hospitality is lacking in almost all of the churches we work with. To gain the perspective of a guest's perception of churches, in 2007 we contracted with an organization called Faith Perceptions. Together, we created twenty-one first impression questions for guests to answer after they experienced worship at one of our churches. Twelve unconnected people were asked to visit the church and then to complete the survey of questions. We learned a great deal from the survey about churches and hospitality. We think we are friendly, but the surveys show that we are not. These surveys have also raised our awareness of other issues, such as the fact that signage is key, the front door is not always the front door, and there are times when guests are simply ignored. It is important to have a hospitality process to recruit, train, and deploy for at least the worship experience, if not all week long. This mystery worshiper process has now been used in more than eighty churches in Missouri. Much of this chapter is based on our learning from those mystery worshiper reports. (For more information on guest hospitality and connections, refer to *Beyond the First Visit* by Gary McIntosh or www.FaithPerceptions.com.)

Once we have implemented the ideas and strategies from Chapter Eight and have people trained and ready to receive guests, we must turn our attention to the facility. We should first be aware that it is highly unlikely for someone to just show up for church. Some come because they have been invited by someone directly or because they are visiting someone who is connected to the church—maybe they are on vacation or visiting for a holiday or family event. Most often, something really big is happening in the life of the guest.

Ninety-seven percent of all newcomers to a church have had a major life transition in the last two months, according to *The Race to Reach Out* by Douglas T. Anderson and Michael J. Coyner (p. 13). They are going through some sort of significant change or challenge. This could be a move, a new baby, the death of a loved one, an illness, entering a ten-step program, a new job, a near-death experience, an accident, or a job loss. The more we are in tune with finding what brings new people to the church, the easier it will be to connect with them. We can build relationships with unconnected people and we can provide ministry that is relevant to them *if* we know what's going on in their lives. There needs to be an intentional process for connecting newcomers with the appropriate people and with the appropriate ministry. We know that new people connect best with other new people. We want guests to feel comfortable and to sense that, if they returned for a second visit, they would be included in the church family. Don't leave the connection process to chance! The intentional process should provide opportunities for members to get to know the guest as well as connect the guest with other newer attenders. In this chapter, we will learn strategies to have a more intentional connection process.

Don't leave the connection process to chance!

Our building footprint matters. So how do you prepare your facility to be inviting to guests? Look at your building through the eyes of a guest. Better yet, invite unconnected guests into your building, walk along with them, and ask them to give you their first impressions of what they see. An outsider perspective is very important. Sometimes the issues are large, but many times, they are a series of small issues that can be resolved easily.

It all starts in the parking lot! Curb appeal matters. Start at the street and work your way into the building. What do you see? What is missing? What needs attention? From the time guests are nearing the arrival at your facility until they leave the grounds, you have multiple opportunities to show hospitality and care toward them, and connection with them. Your building can act as an evangelist or a deterrent. What could you do to freshen up the outside of your building? Let's meander through your facility and worship experience with a checklist of items to consider in preparation for guests. This is certainly not an exhaustive list, but it is sure to help you improve your facility as you build a culture of hospitality.

Remember, we are building a culture of hospitality!

HOSPITALITY CHECKLIST

1. Exterior Signage and Accessibility

How easy is it to identify your building from the road? Is the time of worship clearly displayed and easily read while driving at the speed limit? How easy or difficult is it to find your building from the closest main thoroughfare? Once the building is identified, how easy is it to find where to enter the parking lot? Do you have parking spots designated for guests? Are those spots easily found and near the main entrance? Once parked, how easy is it to find the entrance? If you have multiple entrances, how is the guest to know which entrance to use? Is there an easily accessible spot for people with special needs, such as those with walkers, wheelchairs, babies, and small children, to be dropped off at a door protected from the elements?

2. First Impression of Human Hospitality

Are parking lot attendants helping people to find parking spots? Are those attendants directing guests to the designated guest parking spots? In inclement weather, is there a parking lot attendant available with an umbrella? Is there a greeter at every entrance, inside and outside? Are the greeters trained? Is each greeter extending a friendly, genuine handshake with a pleasant greeting and good eye contact? Is the greeter being distracted into conversations with regular attenders? Is the greeter familiar with the regular attenders so that guests can be identified easily?

3. How to Get Their Names

You need to have multiple methods to acquire guests' names: collecting the names on the guest attendance pads during worship, guest sign-in sheets, a tear-off from the bulletin, parents who sign in their children at the nursery, greeters who are trained to have pen and paper to write names down and turn them in to the office, or congregants getting the names of guests sitting next to them and following up personally on Facebook or with e-mail. This is why it is important to have routine, congregational-wide training on the process of receiving and connecting guests. We make mistakes in our attempts to receive guests. Sometimes we smother them, and other times we unintentionally ignore them. We must create a system in which our guests feel welcome but not overwhelmed. Good, welcoming, authentic conversation is critical, and it can be tricky. What are the best ways to engage a guest in conversation? What conversation starters actually do more harm than good? Following are some conversation starters to engage in, as well as some to steer clear of:

Do's

1. "Hi, I'm (name)." If the guests respond with their names, either you write them down or have the guests write them down on your bulletin. Turn in the names. Follow up with them personally.

2. "Good to see you."

3. "I don't believe I have had the pleasure of meeting you. I'm (name)."

Don'ts

1. "You must be new here."

2. "How long have you been coming here? I've never seen you before."

3. "My name is (first and last name), and what is yours?"

4. Think Guest, Not Visitor

How do you prepare for visitors in your home? We think of visitors as people who drop by without an invitation. They just show up. We are not prepared for them. We might just stand with them in the entrance to visit. We don't want them to see the dirty dishes in the sink, the unmade beds, and the towels on the bathroom floor. The visit is usually short. You may have been disrupted by it.

In contrast, how might you prepare for guests in your home? How does this differ from a visitor? Guests have been invited to your home. You are expecting their arrival. You are most likely looking forward to their time with you. You make special arrangements and preparations for them. You have likely done some extra cleaning. You might have prepared their favorite meal or dessert. You will likely offer them something to drink. You may allow them to sit in your favorite chair. You might even share the remote control with them. (Okay, now you think I am meddling!) If they are spending the night, you have placed fresh linens on the bed and your best towels on the vanity for their use. You are happy to see them and have them in your home, and the stay is usually longer in duration than that of a visitor.

How does this translate to church? Does your church have visitors drop by for worship? Does this take you by surprise, making you wish you had been more ready? Or do you prepare for guests each Sunday? Do you try to make them feel welcome and comfortable? When unconnected guests visit a church, they have a fear that it will be awkward. They are not sure what to expect. We want to ease those concerns as much as possible. We do that with a process and culture of radical hospitality. Remember, radical hospitality is going above and beyond the expectations of hospitality.

5. Connector

Every church needs a connector. What is a connector? A connector is a person or group of people who invest in building relationships with guests and help them "connect" into a ministry where the guests will get their needs met. The connector will keep in contact with and track the guest until the guest becomes a regular attender, gets involved in ministry, and fosters a relationship with Christ through your church's intentional faith development pathway.

Once a greeter has identified a guest, is there a connector available for the guest? Is that connector trained? Is that connector gifted for this responsibility? Does the connector introduce him or herself and escort guests to the hospitality area for a drink or refreshment? Is the connector equipped with questions that are friendly and un-intimidating, while still obtaining necessary information for a follow-up and ultimately a good connection point? Is the connector introducing the guests to others? Does the connector invite the guest to sit with him or her during service? Is the connector assisting the guest in feeling comfortable during the worship experience? Is the connector introducing the guest to the pastor at the conclusion of worship? Does the connector invite the guest to lunch? Does the connector walk away with at least a name, address, and phone number and the reason the guest decided to attend worship? Is the connector aware of the next step in the connection process, and is he or she committed to take that step with this guest?

6. Welcome Center

Does your church have an area where guests can find information about your church and its ministries? Is this welcome center staffed throughout all the Sunday morning activities? Are the people who staff the center well trained in the ministries of the church? Do they understand the importance of connecting with guests? Do they understand the importance of escorting guests to points of interest rather than pointing them in the direction? Do they know who the connectors are in the church and how to "connect" the guest with the connector? Is the welcome center well equipped with updated information about current and ongoing ministries? Is printed information available for guests to take with them?

7. Lobby

Is the area right inside your main entrance warm and inviting? Is the area congested? Does it radiate the welcome feeling of "come on in"? Does it allow for fellowship? Is it up to date in its décor and furnishings? Is there a digital screen easily viewable with information? Is the lobby area free of clutter? What era are the pictures from that are hanging in the lobby? Is there a fresh coat of paint in a modern (non-white) color on the walls? Are there refreshments and coffee available and easily found? Are the furnishings modern and comfortable?

8. Nursery

For guests with young children, this is a critical area. How easy is it to find the nursery? Is it conveniently located in relationship to the sanctuary? Is it clean? Is the furniture updated and safe? Is it child-friendly? Is the décor appealing to the entire family? Is there staff trained with appropriate child-to-caregiver ratios? Has the staff been given a background check? Is the staff trained? Is there a check-in and check-out process? Is there a system to reach parents during worship if they are needed? If so, is that process explained to the parents? Is this a place where you would feel comfortable and safe in leaving your loved one (child, grandchild, niece, or nephew)? If children are first attending service and later taken from the worship area into another area, do the parents know where their children are going and where and when to find them? Are parents prepped for this to occur before it actually happens in order to make an informed and comfortable decision?

9. Pre-Worship Atmosphere

The ten minutes before worship begins and after worship ends are the most critical times for guests. If guests are brave enough to be a few minutes early, this can be an awkward time. What is going on in the sanctuary? Is there soft music playing in the background? Are there videos or other messages displayed on the screen? Are people talking among themselves, or are they inviting guests into conversation? Are guests sitting in an area where no one else is around? Do guests feel like they are in a spotlight? Is the room deathly silent? Is there laughter all around, excluding the guests? Do the guests feel as though they crashed someone else's party? For those who arrive ten minutes after worship begins, is the greeting process still in place? If not, you are going to miss people. Guests arrive early or late, but rarely on time. Be prepared.

10. Meet and Greet

If there is a meet and greet time during worship, how comfortable is it for guests? Does it go longer than two minutes? Do people gravitate to those they already know? Are guests overwhelmed? Are guests ignored? Is this the only time regular attenders pay attention to guests? Are the greetings authentic for guests?

During a consultation weekend, I (Kay) was asked to sit in the front row. I did so by myself. When the meet and greet time came, I turned and greeted the two people behind me. There was no one else closer than three rows away. As I watched the scene unfold alone from the front row, I was simply amazed at what I witnessed. People were actually crisscrossing the sanctuary to greet one another. While it was an incredible scene to observe, I couldn't help but feel awkward standing alone in the front pew for seven minutes! While these folks were being incredibly friendly (to one another), they were blind to the fact that they had left a guest feeling isolated and uncomfortable. If I felt that way, can you imagine how an unconnected "seeker" as a first-time guest might have felt? Do you think he or she would return? Each person in our congregation must be trained to become a personal missionary in the pew.

11. Announcements

If you insist on having announcements, you need to limit them to three minutes or less and thirty seconds or less per announcement. Announcements should pertain to the entire congregation, not just one particular segment or ministry. Otherwise, do not announce it. The larger the congregation, the less effective announcements are from the pulpit. The bullhorn announcements of "you all come" are becoming less and less effective. Are you using insider language that would be intimidating or confusing to an unconnected guest? Are invitations for events clearly defined with who is invited to attend, where the location of the event is (not just "Susie's house"), the cost (if any) to participate, and whether this is a one-time or recurring event? Are you using acronyms that would confuse guests? For example, one church's bulletin noted "Children-KFC" at 4:00 on Sundays. It could be interpreted by a guest that the children met at Kentucky Fried Chicken on Sundays at 4:00. Instead, the children's ministry was named "Kids for Christ."

12. Worship Participation

For an unconnected guest, does your bulletin, multimedia, or worship leadership provide clear directions and understanding? (Remember the use of the word *bulletin* is old language. In other venues, our bulletin would be called a program.) Is it easy for guests to follow along? Are happenings (baptisms, communion, responsive readings) in the service fully explained? Is insider language either not used or fully explained? Do guests know what their expected participation level is? Is the guest ever called out, brought attention to, or made to feel inadequately prepared to participate fully in worship? Is a connector sitting with a guest to help with knowing what to expect and what to do? Is the worship leader introduced?

13. After-Worship Experience

One of the teachings from our mystery worshiper reports is the importance of the guest's experience upon leaving worship. It is just as important as their experience upon arrival. But we rarely pay attention to the guest's departure experience. Remember, any time people have a positive experience, they want to share it with others. This is true of a positive worship experience, too. Once the worship ends, many times the regular attenders go about their business of making lunch plans with their church friends. The unconnected guests are left to fend for themselves. This is a crucial time for guests. Greeters need to be at their stations after worship as well as before. The ten-minute period after service has concluded is a critical time to connect with the guest. Has the guest been introduced to the pastor yet? Invited to lunch? What is the next step? Are you offering tours of the building as an opportunity to show hospitality and engage in more conversation with the guest? Is a gift delivered to the guest's door within the same day as the visit or at least within twenty-four hours? Depending on the needs of the guest, who is the right person or ministry to connect with the guest? Who is responsible for tracking all the guests? What can the church do to be helpful to this person?

It is absolutely critical to follow up within twenty-four to forty-eight hours. Otherwise it feels like "I was a guest but am now not invited back." Let's return to our analogy of hospitality as hosting a guest in our home. After you have invited people to your home, made special arrangements for their visit, enjoyed the time you spent together, and sent them on their way, imagine not ever speaking to them again. No note, no e-mail, no visit. Nothing! When your guests receive no second invitation, it makes them feel that the first visit didn't go well. The guests will likely feel as though they did or said something wrong during their visit, or maybe that it was a one-time-only invitation. Now relate this to the follow-up process in your church. Do guests simply get a form letter? Do they get anything at all? What is the personal touch that gives them a sense of connection and makes them want to return after their first visit? Second visit? Third visit? Remember, everyone is a missionary. Everybody has responsibility for following up with new people, turning the names into the office as well as making a personal connection.

14. Hire Mystery Worshipers

Another great tool to use to prepare the congregation for guests is to contract with a company that sends mystery worshipers to your church. The company will hire unconnected people to attend your church. The mystery worshiper will answer questions and report on the experience. A report of six to twelve mystery worshipers will be compiled. This is a great way to capture guests' complete worship experience through the eyes of the unconnected. We try to evaluate ourselves with our own eyes and ears, but it is much more effective to evaluate through the eyes and ears of those we are trying to reach. The mystery worshiper process is best conducted without the congregation knowing about it. Otherwise, the congregation is on their best behavior and the mystery worshiper's experience is not the same as the typical guest's experience. Your results will be much more authentic and useful if the congregation is unaware of the process.

15. Improve Your Social Media Presence and Impression

In today's world, many people "shop" your church without ever leaving their home, especially the "Three T's": those in their teens, twenties, and thirties. They surf the internet for churches in the area and make decisions on where to "try" based on websites and Facebook alone. So websites are often the first impression for unconnected guests. Decisions are made whether to even try out your church based on the website. Is your website giving the message you want guests to receive? Are your location and worship times clearly indicated on the home page? What is your signature ministry? Is the mission and vision of your church clearly indicated? Are there pictures of your ministries? Is the information up to date? Is there contact information for questions? Can you easily find the staff with pictures and contact information? Your website shouldn't be a bulletin board in a cloud.

Are you using social media to promote your church and attract the unconnected to your ministries? Does your church have a Facebook page? Is it regularly updated? Are you uploading pictures from ministry events to Facebook? Do you use Twitter to update followers? If you don't currently use social media, find a youth or young adult in your church to get this started for you.

> **Your website should not be a bulletin board in the cloud.**

16. Critical Mass

During a recent experience I (Bob) was attending worship in a church where I had never attended before. The sanctuary was only a third full when everyone was seated. This felt empty and did not create an atmosphere where you felt comfortable singing. In your church, how does it feel? If the room is at 80 percent capacity, it will feel full. Is the room comfortably full or awkwardly empty? Do all the insiders sit in the back and nobody up front? Do they all sit on one side? Are they strung all over, where you could shoot off a cannon and hit no one? Are you at or over 80 percent capacity and considering adding another service?

If the room you worship in doesn't create the feeling of critical mass, here are a few strategies you might consider: Take out a few pews in the back to create some lobby or hospitality space. Take out a few pews in front to create more of a stage area. Do some pews need to be removed or shortened to create some special access space? Consider removing pews in the back and replacing them with rocking chairs for new parents. Are there too many worship services for the number attending? If so, consider consolidating worship services to create critical mass. Spread the pews out. The pews are traditionally spaced 18 inches apart. People were smaller when the church was built, so consider removing some pews to allow instead for 24 inches of spacing between pews. You can also use large banners or fabric streamers in the pews to move folks forward and sit nearer to the front and together, especially if the size of the worshiping congregations varies dramatically between services in the same space.

> **Critical mass is extremely important. Too many or too few may hamper unconnected guests from returning.**

Remember, relationships are what we have to offer: our relationship with God and our relationships with one another, as well as our availability to people we do not know. Our relationships are often confirmed through the worship experience. How worship goes is often how the rest of church goes. If our worship is not very engaging, it is doubtful the church will be very engaging. In the next chapter, we will learn how to move beyond friendliness to friendships and into discipleship.

10

RELATIONSHIPS MATTER

Every church we have consulted with is convinced that it is the friendliest church in town. We often tease church leaders by saying we have yet to meet the un-friendliest church in town! Many times we pride ourselves in just how friendly we are. But unconnected guests in our churches are looking for friendships, not just friendly people. They are looking for relationships. This is a vital distinction. It is one thing to put on our Christian smile each Sunday and be polite. But it is quite another thing to be genuinely interested in people and have a desire to help them know and love Jesus Christ. Interestingly enough, a mystery worshiper once reported that the church he had visited was indeed friendly, but it was quite apparent in the handshakes and small talk that these folks were not looking to invest in new friendships. To become missionaries of Jesus Christ, it may be necessary from time to time to move away from our current relationships with our Christian friends and invest in new relationships with unconnected people so that we may help others begin to walk with Christ. Although this is obviously difficult, as mature Christians, we are called to spread the Good News. One of the disciplines of a disciple of Jesus Christ is to create margins in one's life in order to establish relationships with people we do not know, the unconnected, therefore becoming missionaries.

We are therefore Christ's ambassadors, as though God were making his appeal through us. We implore you on Christ's behalf: Be reconciled to God.—2 Corinthians 5:20 NIV

While we have been talking mostly up to this point about how to create a culture of hospitality, we must also have a formal process of hospitality and connection. There are four distinct steps in the process of moving an unconnected guest from a relationship-building event or conversation to life as a follower of Christ:

- Step One: From Outsider to Guest
  - ○ Phase One: Prayer
  - ○ Phase Two: Bridge Events
  - ○ Phase Three: Follow Up
- Step Two: From Guest to Connected
- Step Three: From Connected to Disciple
- Step Four: From Disciple to Ambassador or Missionary

STEP ONE: FROM OUTSIDER TO GUEST

Phase One: Prayer

Phase One of the first step is to establish a prayer ministry. Now, this prayer team is most likely very different from the prayer teams you currently have or have had in your church. This prayer team is outwardly focused. They are praying for the leaders in the community: the police, the fire personnel, principals, teachers, and superintendents, as well as those unconnected who are lost and searching for a better life. We many times have a prayer chain or prayer group in our churches, but they typically focus on the joys and concerns of those already connected with the church. This new ministry will have a new focus—the mission field! This team will pray unconnected people into church. They will pray that the congregation will be the pathway for the unconnected to find a relationship with Christ. They will pray that the ministries of the church allow for the unconnected to become a part of the faith community. They will pray for the church bridge events in Phase Two (before, during, and after). This prayer team will pray for the event and even walk around the event silently praying for the attendees and workers. This team will pray with and for the pastor before each worship service. Who are the prayer warriors in your church? How might you invite them to be a part of the life of the church?

Phase Two: Bridge Events

Bridge events are conducted outside the church walls and preferably off church property. We suggest hosting three bridge events a year, two off church property and one on the church property. If you are just starting, do one. Do it right, do it big, and do it well. Make sure you pray the event in. Make sure you follow up. We want to remove all potential barriers for unconnected people to experience church in a whole new way. Therefore, the event should be a "P-Free Zone." No Preaching. No Prayers. No Pressure. No Pocketbooks. This bridge event should be something that is needed by the community or something unconnected people in the community will enjoy. Three essential elements for a bridge event are radical hospitality, a means to collect names, and fun! Just as we have hospitality teams trained and ready to go for worship, we must deploy these same teams at bridge events. It is their job to mingle to make sure people are enjoying themselves, feeling welcome, engaged in light conversation, and receiving a true sense of appreciation for their attendance. We have learned to share our story in safe places and with people we don't know. Bridge events are an excellent place to extend an invitation to these same people we have been working to engage in the community.

Here is a possible list of bridge events for your consideration:

1. Community trick or treat
2. Concert in the park
3. Bike (motorcycle) night/show
4. Auto show
5. Craft show
6. Bike safety clinic
7. Child seat safety checks
8. Community egg hunt
9. Carnival
10. Community play day
11. Free community swim at local pool
12. Sponsor booth at community fair with diaper changing or nursing station
13. Free lunch in a park for kids during the summer

14. School supply giveaway

15. Clothing giveaway for school children

16. Free coat giveaway

17. Free parenting classes

18. Free financial classes

Remember, have some fun!

Phase Three: Follow Up

It is essential to find ways to get unconnected people's names unobtrusively and to follow up. It does not do us any good to have a big bridge event and get no names. Getting names is tricky and will require some brainstorming. You need to brainstorm a variety of ways to do it. You won't get all the names, but you will get some. Note: you must have a follow-up team. This follow-up team is critical to the process. If we don't follow up with the people who attended, all our work was most likely done in vain. If there is no connection with people, they are unlikely to show up at worship or any other church ministry. Remember, the purpose of a bridge-building event is to create opportunities to build relationships with unconnected people we do not know in our mission field, so that we might have the opportunity to build an authentic relationship that may lead to a faith conversation, which may lead them back to our faith community.

One name-collecting method involves giving away a gift that really appeals to the people attending the event. This could be a gift certificate to an event, a local store, a grocery store, or something in alignment with the event. For example, you could give away a bike at a children's bike safety check event. You could give away an iPad at the community financial seminar. Collect people's names and contact information, put them in one box or hat (or whatever is fun and makes sense for the event), and then draw the prize winners from the collected names. Be creative!

Another way to collect names is to have connector people wandering through the event. Connectors write down the names of those people they meet and turn the names in to the event organizer, church office, and prayer team. They personally follow up with guests they met during the event. Hold connectors accountable for this follow-up. The prayer team should pray for the unconnected guests who attend the bridge event.

Usually, the real time and energy go into the planning of the bridge event. Once the event is over, we put the names in a spreadsheet and pat ourselves on the back for a job well done. The end. Let us challenge you a bit on this. When the bridge event is over, the work really begins. We must be very careful in how we are using the resources (time, talents, energy, dollars, passion, and so on) of our church. We spend our resources on the event itself and then have nothing to invest in the follow-up. Or we spend our time fellowshipping with one another at the bridge event instead of being focused on the purpose of the event, which is the opportunity to start building relationships with unconnected people.

When the bridge event is over, the work really begins.

The follow-up team will kick into high gear after a bridge event. This is when the real work begins. The names collected at the event are divided among the team. The team sends handwritten notes to each guest, thanking them for attending the event. The person writing the note should also introduce himself or herself as the guest's prayer partner. The team member should consistently pray for the event attendee and, over the course of a few weeks, handwrite two or three more notes to the guest, offering assistance and kind words. Note: the first correspondence should be sent out within twenty-four to forty-eight hours of the event. After a few handwritten notes are sent, the team members should phone the guests. The purpose is to introduce themselves and to see if there is anything the team members or church can do to be of assistance. Exchange kind words and ask questions to show authentic concern and desire to know the person. After a few phone calls, send e-mails or connect on Facebook. Inquire whether the guests have a church family and attend regularly. If they do not, invite them to be "guests" at church on Sunday and offer a ride or to meet them. This process invests in people and authentic relationships. This follow-up process must be intentional, and team members must be held accountable for the follow-up process.

People don't often give us their names. They don't want to give us their names because they don't want us to sell them something. We are but a stranger to them if we do not invest in connecting with them on any level. For people to be willing to give us their contact information, we must first begin to build authentic relationships.

STEP TWO: FROM GUEST TO CONNECTED

We all need and desire fellowship with our friends. It is a great part of being a faith community. Where fellowship becomes a problem is when it is the only type of relationship occurring at our church. Fellowship is about engaging with people we already know—the connected. When we begin to turn our hearts outward, we begin to see that fellowship is very inwardly focused. Hospitality occurs when we turn those conversations and connections to our unconnected guests. Radical hospitality is fellowship turned outward toward those who are unconnected. Hospitality is the opportunity for people to see Christ through our actions and deeds. Does your church engage in only fellowship, or do you have a culture of radical hospitality, too?

Once unconnected guests have entered our church doors, we must have an intentional process of connecting them into the life of the congregation. To do this, we must get to know them and their needs. The connector (described earlier) will be responsible for the follow-up process and for tracking how the guests might grow in their faith. Every church should know the three easiest ways to connect new people into the life of the congregation. If the guests have had a prayer partner, the prayer partner should be updating the connector with information about the guest and their needs. Every congregation needs to have a process in place in which the pastor, staff, and leaders meet together to ensure that all new people have prayer partners and connectors assigned. One way to do this is to have a short meeting with key leaders on Monday morning to make sure guests are assigned a prayer partner and connector and to double check on the previous week's guests. Every board meeting should include a time of ensuring that every new guest we have received since the last meeting has received a prayer partner and connector. Make new people the priority.

> **Make new people a priority.**

The connectors in the church should have some sort of tracking system that saves all the guest information, including who their connector is, dates of visits, guests' needs, and people/groups/information that the guest has been connected with. The connector will want to spend some one-on-one time getting to know the unconnected guest. Key questions should be identified to get to the real needs of the guest. Many times, those first one-on-one visits are designed to share all about the church with the guest, to "sell the church" effectively. We want to turn that model upside down and be intentional about concentrating those visits on finding out more about the unconnected guests and their needs. The connector should introduce the unconnected guests to leaders of small groups or ministries where the guests might connect based on their needs, desires, or interests. This could be a small (covenant) group, choir, mission trip, or short-term class. The connector should check in with the leaders to make sure the guests continue to engage and attend the connection points. If they are not attending, the connector should visit with the unconnected guests again to see if there is a better fit (connection point) for the guests in a different ministry of the church.

The goal of the connector is to take a person from being an unconnected guest to a regular attender. The timeline for this process will vary from person to person. The length of the process depends in part on how quickly the person finds a suitable group or ministry to be involved in. This may happen on the first "connection," or it may take multiple connection tries to find a good fit. Remember, most people decide if our church will become their church within three months of first attending, so connecting them quickly and effectively is extremely important.

Within those first twenty-four to forty-eight hours after an unconnected guest's first visit to worship, consider a screen door visit and a call from the pastor. The visit may occur on Sunday and the call on Monday. The visit should be conducted by trained laity. It is a quick visit at the person's front door. It is not intended to be a visit inside the home. It is a quick thank you for coming and extending a gift as a token of appreciation for their attendance. Don't be pushy. Don't stay more than a minute or two. Don't push the church. Just let them know it was a pleasure to have them as guests today and express hope that they will return next week. Ask them if there is anything you could do to be helpful. Other connections should include Facebook, e-mail, or Twitter.

> **New people connect best with other new people!**

STEP THREE: FROM CONNECTED TO DISCIPLE

Once an unconnected person becomes a regular attender and is well connected in a ministry, it is time to move that person onto a discipleship pathway. The ministry hopefully has a means of connecting people to that pathway. If not, the connector, pastor or another process will need to make sure this happens. This is a critical step. We must make sure we engage people in an intentional process to develop their faith continuously. The connection process is not completed until the person has successfully moved from being an unconnected guest to becoming a disciple.

Now that we have moved unconnected people into a desire to grow their faith on a continuous basis, we must offer the opportunity for them to grow their faith. Faith development does not happen by osmosis. Just because someone has sat in the pews for decades does not automatically make that person a disciple. The church must provide a pathway for all to grow in their faith. We are never finished growing in our relationship with Christ. It must be an intentional process that offers opportunities for us to grow, be challenged, and become more Christ-like. We are continually growing and maturing in our faith in Jesus Christ and one another.

> **We must have an intentional pathway to grow our faith.**

Many times we get caught up in throwing out studies or curricula for groups in our church to study without knowing what the goal is. For instance, how would you describe an authentic follower of Jesus Christ? We should know the desired end before we begin. We must understand that a discipleship pathway is NOT a curriculum. An intentional faith development process or pathway is a clear picture of the characteristics, knowledge, actions, behaviors, and attributes that make up a mature disciple. It is not only a step-by-step process. It is knowing what the steps are but also knowing that not everybody takes the same steps. People need to move freely within the process, depending on their needs and their relationship with Christ. The process likely will not change, but the opportunities available to help disciples move along in their faith development will change from time to time. Small groups are an important part of this discipleship process.

There are many different models of intentional faith development processes. There is no one right way or perfect pathway. The idea is to have an intentional process that allows and creates an expectation of continual growth.

A faith development pathway could be based on the character traits of Jesus and include opportunities to grow closer to Jesus' example. It could be described as an intentional process of daily living out our membership vows. Another option is to use the *Five Practices of Fruitful Living* by Bishop Robert Schnase, engaging people in those practices. *Simple Church* by Eric Geiger offers a discipleship pathway that is simple and easy to follow. Another model worth considering is the one developed by the Church of the Resurrection in Leawood, Kansas, called "The Journey." This model has three main sections: Knowing God, Loving God, and Serving God. Visit COR.org for more information.

You might develop your own step-by-step process of some kind, using one of the other excellent resources available. The intentional discipleship pathway creates a means for people to practice authentic discipleship, so that they become more like Christ and so that they go out into the world as agents of kingdom change. The discipleship pathway also ensures that these practices define us corporately, as the collected body of Christ.

There are many options, but the important thing is for your church to develop and follow an intentional process to grow disciples. What would happen if we expected no specific outcomes from our children's education? Would we send our kids to school, assuming something might happen, without any sort of plan for what *should* happen? Without any sort of plan for *how* it would happen? In that case, we could have no expectations for our children to learn anything in particular at all. In our consulting work, we have yet to walk into a church that had a discipleship pathway in place. We must do better by our congregations if we are to develop authentic, mature disciples of Christ.

STEP FOUR: FROM DISCIPLE TO AMBASSADOR OR MISSIONARY

While we are never finished with our faith development here on Earth, we do hopefully move into a matured disciple phase. That phase is becoming a missionary. As we continue to move toward being more Christ-like, we also take on the task, or better yet the lifestyle, of being Christ's ambassador. As ambassadors, we see it as our responsibility and privilege to be the conduit for others to discover a relationship with Christ. As missionaries for Christ, we are honored to be evangelists in our congregations and in the mission field to which Christ has called us. We are practicing graduate evangelism on a regular basis, while continuing to deepen our own faith, as we continue throughout our lives on our intentional discipleship pathway. We are modeling a missionary lifestyle and mentoring the next generation of missionaries.

In this section, we have learned how important it is to build the church's corporate foundation to create a culture of radical hospitality and to equip leaders. We learned how to prepare our facilities for hospitality and for unconnected guests every week and every day. We discovered how to train teams and our entire congregation with intentional processes to prepare for guests, to create a culture of radical hospitality. We learned how to implement strategies and events to connect with the unconnected. This section concluded with understanding why an intentional faith development process is important and the elements we must include in creating that pathway to take someone from an unconnected stranger to Christ's ambassador.

EPILOGUE

The idea of reaching people we do not know is not a Farr, Kotan, Anderson idea. The idea of reaching people we do not know for the sake of Jesus Christ is inherently a biblical idea. One of the Bible's themes is that God wants to reach people. And throughout history, God has always used people to reach other people. God is not an isolated God. God thrives in community. The very nature of God is the Trinity. Three in one. One in three. Community and mystery. Let us walk through the Bible briefly to identify this theme of reaching new people.

Genesis 1: God created people, called them good, and blessed them with abundance. God wants good things for all people.

Genesis 3: We human beings always think we know better. And we decide it is all about us. Otherwise known as the great fall or the great sin.

Genesis 7: God creates a new thing. We called it the great flood. Noah is selected to do a new thing and raise up new people.

Genesis 12: God selects Abraham to do a new thing and raise up new people.

1 Kings 10: God selects kings, the most famous of whom are David and Solomon, to do a new thing and raise up a new people.

Isaiah 49: This time God sends prophets, some of them minor and some of them major, to shout into the desert, to do a new thing and raise up a new people because the people have not listened.

Luke 2: God takes a radical step and sends God's only begotten son. To do what? To do a new thing and raise up a new people.

Matthew 16: Jesus does pretty well until he attends the finance committee meeting and tells them he is going to do a new thing and raise up a new people. The people in power decide no way! They did what people always do and made it all about them. They forgot the mission. They took matters into their own hands. Within three weeks, Jesus is dead on the tree.

Matthew 28: Jesus comes back to everyone's surprise and tells them to go into all the world and do a new thing and raise up a new people.

Acts 9 and Ephesians 2: The clergy have decided it is all about them. They forget the mission. And they determine this new thing is only for the Jewish Christians. But the Apostle Paul and the Holy Spirit remind everyone that all are missionaries and all are gifts of God. We call this the priesthood of all believers. It is about the mission.

Revelation 5: At the end of the day, it is God's desire that every people and all persons come home to God. Every knee bows and every tongue confesses that Jesus Christ is Lord and Savior.

In this quick skimming of the Bible, you will notice a theme. God wants to reach new people and do a new thing. You also will notice that about every five hundred years or so, God has to raise up a new people to do a new thing. because those who had been handed the mantle decided it was all about them and forgot the mission.

Just for a moment, think back five hundred years. Where does that place us? In the Protestant reformation! God raised up a man named Luther and told him to do a new thing and raise up a new people. The Protestant Reformation produced our mainline denominations. So here we are with all the old methods not working and a very inwardly focused church. And we believe God is trying to raise up a new people to do a new thing.

Are you willing to be in the new movement, to be a new people, to do a new thing? Are you willing to put a candle on the light stand for all to see and take it out from underneath the bushel basket where only those who know can see? *Get their name.* Start a conversation, Build an authentic relationship that leads to the possibility for a faith conversation that might lead someone into the faith community of God. Remember, God desperately loves you, and God desperately loves all the world. So, *get their name!* Write it down. Follow Up. And go beyond creating new relationships between ourselves, others,

God and the community of faith. Never forget the mission: "making new disciples of Jesus Christ for the transformation of the world."

It is our prayers that this book will be a helpful tool to get your church out of the building and into the mission field.

Bob, Doug & Kay